"I just got a job in sales! Now what?"
A Playbook for Skyrocketing Your Commissions

By Todd Natenberg
President
TBN Sales Solutions

CP Publishing • Chicago, IL

To Steve,

Sell how
you want
to live!

Todd
Mailloux
9/15/04

Praise for

"I just got a job in sales. Now what?"
A Playbook for Skyrocketing Your Commissions

What the experts say ...

"This powerful, practical, fast-moving book gives you a series of proven techniques you can use to get your sales career off to a fast start."

Brian Tracy, Author of *Turbo Strategy*

"If you just got a job in sales, then you just better buy this book. Rather than 'just got a job,' you'll 'just make some sales.' This book informs, inspires, and presents practical real-world information that converts sales goals to sales contracts."

Jeffrey Gitomer, Author of *The Sales Bible*

"Not only is this a must read for new salespeople, it's a terrific solution for an experienced salesperson in a slump who needs to get back to basics."

Roger Dawson, Author of *Secrets of Power Negotiating for Salespeople*

"Awesome! Todd's playbook is more than theory – it contains a wealth of valuable, practical ideas. Told from the perspective of someone who has learned the job inside and out, his book should be required reading for anyone starting out in the field of sales."

Stephan Schiffman, President of DEI Management Group, who has been cited as the foremost expert in the area of Prospecting Skills and is internationally known as "America's #1 Corporate Sales Trainer"

"A compelling book. Without question, this will be an important and useful book for anyone serious about improving their sales performance."

Gerald L. Manning, Author of *Selling Today – Creating Customer Value*

(Continued on next page)

"I just got a job in sales! Now what?"
A Playbook for Skyrocketing Your Commissions

What the experts say ...

"Todd writes from the perspective of someone who still lives the life of the salesperson today and who truly understands the sales process. If you are looking to break into sales or are new to sales, do not put off reading this book."

Rita Emmett, Author of *The Procrastinator's Handbook*

"Todd's enthusiasm for sales and the selling process invokes excitement even in those who dread cold calls. You can feel his passion and fervor on every page."

Lillian D. Bjorseth, Author of *Breakthrough Networking: Building Relationships That Last*

"This book is different. Reading it could give you an edge that makes a difference."

Jim Meisenheimer, Sales Strategist

What the readers say ...

"Todd hits the nail on the head! This is not just quick tips to inspire and motivate reps for a moment. I just got a job in sales! Now what? *establishes a sales process from A to Z. Todd's insight and commitment to the sales profession is one that will result in a huge success for all readers."*

David Hackett, Sales Manager, Qwest Communications

"This is a real hands-on book that helps with the fundamentals. It will help the newer salespeople accelerate their learning curve and it will help the good salespeople become top performers."

Paul Rosen, Vice President of Sales and Marketing, E-Chx, Inc.

"In three short months after reading your book and going through your training, I can say my commissions have increased about 15%. My weekly activity has increased 20%.

I have gained many insights into learning how to increase my business. My business is taking shape through several great ways. By organizing my time, I am conscious of the time I spend every day. With your guidance, I am more efficiently tracking the way I spend my time. Activity has increased three-fold. By organizing my most important to least important activities, I can say my efficiency has increased. In using the PALs and sending e-mail to my prospective clients, I have closed more sales."

Eric Marzinke, Financial Consultant, AXA Advisors

"This book defined all the lessons I had to learn the hard way in sales and provides a great roadmap as I move through my career. I consider this a must-read for anyone working in sales. If you are at the beginning, middle or end of your career, this book defines the behaviors of the top tier sales professionals."

Erik A. Carlsen, Document Management Consultant
IKON Office Solutions

Attention Professional Organizations, Associations, Corporations, Universities and Colleges:

Quantity discounts are available for bulk purchases of this book for educational, gift purposes or as premiums for increasing membership, renewals or magazine subscriptions. Special books or book excerpts can also be created to fit special needs.

For more information, please contact TBN Sales Solutions, 866-464-0339 or e-mail todd@toddnatenberg.com.

For Claudia,
for all her love and support

©2003 by Todd Natenberg

TBN Sales Solutions
711 W. Gordon Terrace, Ste. 106, Chicago, IL 60613
866-464-0339
todd@toddnatenberg.com
www.ijustgotajobinsales.com

Cover photo	Larry Reiss
Cover design	David Nissim-Sabbat, Internet Horizons (www.internethorizons.com)
Book editor & Graphic design	Deb Manning (www.debmanning.com)

Natenberg, Todd
"I just got a job in sales. Now what?" A Playbook for Skyrocketing Your
Commissions"

Printed in Canada

ISBN#0-9743469-1-8

CP Publishing
Chicago, IL

ABOUT THE AUTHOR

As the president and founder of TBN Sales Solutions (TBNSS), Todd earns new clients and delivers customized sales training. By establishing universal structures in all facets of sales processes, he leads TBNSS to excel in developing training focused on sales commissions and improving retention rates of employees.

Prior to TBNSS, Todd was a sales manager and regional sales trainer for Teligent, Inc., in Chicago, a full service integrated provider offering local, long distance and data services nationwide. As the company's first Midwest Regional Sales Trainer, Todd taught sales teams in Chicago, Denver, Milwaukee and Cleveland. He conducted new hire training and wrote Teligent's first sales presentations.

Todd's telecommunications career originally began with LCI International in Chicago. In addition to LCI, he was a top salesperson at AT&T and USN Communications. Previously, he sold photocopiers and faxes.

A graduate of the University of Missouri-Columbia School of Journalism, Todd began his career as a newspaper reporter. He served a Pulliam Fellowship at *The Arizona Republic* in Phoenix and was a staff writer for the *Daily Herald,* a newspaper in suburban Chicago. He still contributes regularly to various sales magazines including *Selling!* and *Sales and Marketing Executive Report.* His first book, *The Journey Within: Two Months on Kibbutz,* was released last year. It chronicles his adventures volunteering on an Israeli kibbutz in the summer of 2000.

In addition to sales training, Todd is a motivational speaker who talks to groups and organizations about self-discovery and personal growth.

Visit www.toddnatenberg.com to learn more about TBN Sales Solutions. You also can contact Todd at 866-464-0339 or e-mail todd@toddnatenberg.com.

Acknowledgements

Ten years ago, if someone had asked me where I'd be today, the last place I would have ever guessed would be owning a sales training company. As a former newspaper reporter, authoring my second book may have been in my plans – but teaching sales skills would have been a stretch.

But one thing sales has taught me is that everything happens for a reason. Now I realize that journalism provided a perfect training ground for learning sales. The similarities between developing a "beat" and a "territory" are amazing. Persistence, establishing trust and having a goal in mind are cornerstones in journalism and sales – and life, as well.

Today, I honestly believe sales to be the greatest profession in the world. When you master the art of sales, you master the art of living. I have many people to thank for helping this mastery come about.

First and foremost, thanks to all my clients. Were it not for you, this book would never have been possible. By serving each of your needs I learned to develop the keys to sales.

Specifically, I'd like to thank Bryan Wadsworth of Wadsworth Pumps and Mark Cleaver of Technomic International. They first entrusted me with their phone service and then with their employees. I was honored to teach them sales skills.

I thank my past mentors, including David Hackett, former sales manager with LCI International and now manager with Qwest Communications, and Bill Ohlhaber, former sales manager with Canon/Ambassador Office Equipment, for their patience and knowledge. In addition, thanks to Ted Ergo, former director of training with USN Communications, and Steve St. John, owner of NTP, Inc. It may have taken time, but now I recognize how much I *really* learned from each of you.

Thanks, also, to the members of the National Speakers Association. While my teachers and mentors change, all members have common traits. They are dedicated individuals who willingly share their expertise, asking only that I pass on their valuable information.

Special thanks, in particular, to Lillian Bjorseth, author of *Breakthrough Networking: Developing Relationships That Last.* Over the past year she has been there more than once to answer my questions. I'm proud to call her a friend.

Thanks also to business humorist Todd Hunt, always eager to lend a helping hand whether in authoring books or fine-tuning workshops. Your support is appreciated.

Thanks to my editor, Debbie Manning. You were terrific. Your "challenging" of each page, theory and wording has produced a book which will make us all proud. Thanks for your diligence and tremendous effort.

To Todd Bermont, author of *10 Insider Secrets to Job Hunting* … thank you for your advice and guidance in the world of publishing – with a special note of gratitude for coming up with the title of this book, *"I just got a job in sales! Now what?"*

To all the authors who have helped me, your support has been invaluable. Specific thanks to Dan Seidman, author of *Death of 20th Century Selling,* Steve White, author of *Family Vacations and Other Hazards of Growing Up,* and Brian King, author of *Everybody Has a Tumor.*

To the many sales trainers and teachers I have had the good fortune of working with and learning from, this book is a compilation of everything you have taught me: Brian Tracy, Tony Robbins, Stephan Schiffman, Jeffrey Gitomer and many more. Had you not created the foundation, none of us would be teaching sales skills today.

And to all salespeople out there today – and those who *think* they want to sell – I thank each of you for being a member of the greatest profession in the world.

Happy selling!

"The most successful people I know are the most successful salespeople I know."

Todd B. Natenberg
President, TBN Sales Solutions

Table of Contents

FOREWORD

John was a 25-year-old newspaper reporter who had enough of the grueling life of a journalist after a mere five years. He believed his hard-nosed investigative skills made a difference in the world ... but his success was accompanied by personal sacrifice. His long working hours estranged him from his future wife. His career's unpredictability, in terms of both financial gain and long-term security, wore on him. John enjoyed helping others, but without the financial freedom he desired, he questioned how he could maximize his potential.

John longed for a career where he could control his own destiny. He yearned to receive a paycheck directly proportionate to the effort he put in and the talent he possessed. John wanted to be his own boss, but still wanted an employer to provide health insurance, office supplies and support in times of trouble.

Does such a profession exist? Could John find a job where he could apply his communication skills and be rewarded with the paycheck he desired? Could he have a job with the ability to continually grow personally and professionally? Could he find a job where he could determine his own hours ... and the responsibility for success and failure would remain in his own hands?

"I know," John said one day. "I'll get a job in sales!"

Within two months, John found a sales job that he thought would work for him. After interviewing for positions selling photocopiers, telecommunications services and payroll services, he found an opportunity that excited him. John would sell local and long distance phone solutions to businesses. He would be part of the booming, but volatile, life of technology sales. He would find new clients. He would be judged on whether he obtained a monthly sales revenue target in new

business, otherwise known as a quota. This quota would determine how much he made in commissions. He would have the
potential to win fancy trips to exotic places and participate in
sales contests. He would have the opportunity to earn much
more than the menial raises he annually faced in journalism.
He would not have to be promoted to earn increases in pay.
John would control his own destiny. The more he succeeded,
the more he would earn. His performance would directly affect
his income. John couldn't wait to get started!

But on the first day on the job, something did not feel right.
John was hesitant. Despite promises from managers and other
company salespeople assuring him that the world was his
oyster, John arrived at work worrying. He suddenly recognized
there was a flip side to the benefits of sales. Unlike in some
professions, John could not have "off" days. While he could
work 20 hours per week and make 10 times more than he ever
had in journalism, he also might work 100 hours per week. And,
if he was not successful, he could make ten times less. "Off"
days would cost him money. John knew the tradeoff was worth
it, but he was frightened.

"I just got a job in sales!" he said aloud. "Now what?"

W hat makes a great salesperson? What separates salespeople who are regularly at the President's Club from
those who barely make ends meet? Is it luck? Is it
hard work? If you are a "people person," does that mean you
will always star as a salesperson? Certain skills and attributes
are necessary to thrive in the sales world which is filled with
frequent rejection, communication dilemmas and constant
pressure to obtain revenue targets. But succeeding in sales goes
well beyond developing simple skills. Sales success involves
applying those skills systematically and methodically to achieve
a targeted objective.

The success of a salesperson comes down to one word: Process.

Success involves understanding what it takes to succeed and then applying that process to what you plan to do. Sales is about sticking to a process – in good times and in bad.

Did you ever play Blackjack at a casino? Have you seen the person who hits on 16 when the dealer has a 6 showing? Nine times out of 10, the individual busts beyond 21 resulting in a losing hand. The dealer, however, has no choice when he hits on 16. The casino has given him strict rules – a process. By a miraculous twist of fate, the dealer gets a five! 21! Everyone at the table loses. But not only do they lose ... the other players then lambaste the individual who hit on 16.

"You didn't follow the rules!" a fellow player says. "If you just stuck with the process, we all would have won."

Of course, Blackjack does not always happen this way, but it is a game oriented to playing the odds. And the fact is the largest percentage of cards in the deck have a 10 value. Therefore, the chance of obtaining a 10 is great.

Football teams have playbooks. Basketball teams have offenses. The military has a war plan. If the great golfer Tiger Woods swings the exact same way every time from the tee-box, the result would be a 300-yard shot down the middle of the fairway the overwhelming majority of the time.

Selling is no different. To be the best of the best, you need a playbook. You need a formula for success. When that formula is established, it must be followed. You can tweak your plan from time to time as outside obstacles and situations call for occasional changes. But, as a whole, you need a process – the correct process – to get you where you want to go.

What is the correct sales process?

Selling comes down to two critical philosophies:

- *Customers do not care how much you know until they know how much you care.*

- *Sell how you want to buy.*

Successful selling is more than determining how many appointments you need to run on a daily, weekly and monthly basis. It's not about fancy ways to close deals. It's not about knowing your product inside and out. All play a role, but to succeed in sales at the level you desire, you need to realize your process. You need to analyze every successful sales action you perform, to the most miniscule of details.

This ability to analyze – to dissect – a successful sales pattern is what separates *"I just got a job in sales! Now what?"* from every other sales book on the market.

You will learn – from A to Z – how to sell. *"I just got a job in sales! Now what?"* is math, algebra and calculus combined. It is the ultimate flowchart. If this happens, do that. If that happens, say this. Before you say anything, do this. This playbook will break down, piece by piece, the art of selling by diagramming outcomes based on certain behaviors. *"I just got a job in sales! Now what?"* will be your reference guide throughout your sales career. It will serve as the ultimate resource in good times as well as bad. Most importantly, this book will achieve **measurable results**.

Every philosophy, technique and strategy that is discussed in *"I just got a job in sales! Now what?"* is used at TBN Sales Solutions on a daily, weekly and monthly basis. We have been implementing these techniques successfully for over 10 years.

"I just got a job in sales! Now what?" is written from the perspective of someone who has lived the life of a salesperson. I

have experienced the ups and downs of sales. I have worked as a salesperson, sales manager and sales trainer in corporate America.

Like John, I am a former newspaper reporter, having graduated from the University of Missouri School of Journalism. I was a journalist for five years, writing for the *Daily Herald* in suburban Chicago, *The Arizona Republic* in Phoenix and *The Kansas City Star.* I have written articles for *The Chicago Tribune* and *Selling!* magazine. Ten years ago, I left journalism to pursue a career in sales. I have never looked back.

I also have worked as a master of ceremonies for a professional football team in Chicago and as a mascot escort for the Chicago Bulls. I have been a Chicago Cubs vendor and referee for men's and co-ed football leagues. I ran the Chicago marathon and volunteered on an Israeli Kibbutz.

As you can see, like you, I have many facets to my life. I sincerely believe that the philosophies of selling can be successfully applied to all aspects of life.

Today, I live the life of the salesperson. I, too, need to earn clients regularly in an effort to skyrocket sales. I cold call, telemarket, network and obtain referrals. Daily, I overcome objections and plan my schedule. When I follow the process, I succeed. When I don't, I fail.

Much of what you read in this book will reinforce what you probably already know, but possibly don't utilize. Hopefully, there will be new topics that will strike you as revolutionary. I want to reiterate just how much I believe in these principles. I will give you a money-back guarantee:

If you do not discover 10 specific strategies that will make you money over the next 220 pages, call me for a full refund!

> *"One of the reasons mature people stop learning is that they become less and less willing to risk failure."*
>
> John Gardner

Let's begin.

Todd B. Natenberg

THE 10 STEP SELLING PROCESS

1. Set Goals

2. Schedule

3. State Initial Benefit

4. Prospect

5. Obtain Referrals

6. Build the Business Case

7. Follow-up

8. Overcome Objections

9. Network

10. Professional Development

CHAPTER 1

Set Goals

Goals: Everything you desire, deserve and need to lead a fulfilled life

You can't get where you are going if you do not know where you want to be. If you do not know where you want to be, no roadmap will get you there.

S uccess comes from purpose. Until you recognize what it is you want to accomplish, you will lack the motivation necessary to accomplish anything. Sales reps burn out easily because they repeatedly ask themselves, "What does it all mean? Why am I doing this?" They lack vision. They can't visualize the pot of gold at the end of the rainbow, because they don't know what the pot of gold looks like.

Work to live. Don't live to work.

If you don't define "living" clearly, how do you know if you're successful at it?
Set goals.

In this chapter, we will present the playbook for setting goals:

1. Write goals down and post them.

2. Make goals measurable.

3. Set deadlines for goals.

4. Make personal and professional goals.

5. Visualize goals.

6. Celebrate goals upon accomplishment.

Write goals down and post them

Do you know why people love e-mail? They can see the words. When people see things, they become real. Until a visual picture is created, it's an idea open to interpretation. With e-mail, there is no room for confusion. People know what the message is, when it was sent, who received the message and who sent the message. Even for those of us with bad memories, the information can be re-read by accessing a computer.

Goals are the same. When goals are written down, they magically become real. They remind salespeople why they endure constant abuse from angry prospects, the pressures of obtaining a monthly quota and continual bantering from managers to close deals. Writing down goals lets you see the pot of gold at the end of your rainbow.

In addition to writing your goals, post them where you will see them regularly – in your office, your home and somewhere visible in the car. Don't worry about overkill. Remind yourself constantly of your goals – the things you desire, deserve and need to lead a fulfilled life.

"Everyone has a success mechanism and a failure mechanism. The failure mechanism goes off by itself. The success mechanism only goes off with a goal. Every time we write down and talk about a goal, we push the button to start the success mechanism."

Charles "Tremendous" Jones, Motivational Speaker & Author

Make goals measurable

Selling 150% of quota, running 10 new sales appointments a week, buying a $65,000 Lexus and owning a $500,000 house with 5-bedrooms and a 3-car garage are all legitimate goals.

"Being happy" is not a goal. "Enjoying life" is not a goal. "Selling a lot" is not a goal. How will you know when you are happy? How will you know when you are enjoying life? What is "a lot?"

Remember Journalist John? When John wrote, the quality of his articles was open to interpretation. This is not the case in sales. Subjectivity does not exist. Selling is based on numbers. Salespeople succeed when they sell. They fail when they don't. Even more specifically, salespeople achieve a certain level of success or failure based on an exact number. Personal goals must be established the same way.

You can't manage what you can't measure. You can't grow what you can't manage.

Set deadlines for your goals

When are you the most productive? When do you get the most amount of work done in the least amount of time?

Usually it's the day before you leave for vacation!

Why? You have no choice. You have no time to think. You just act. You have to focus, so nothing holds you back. You remove all obstacles because of the urgency. Why is the urgency so great? It's because the consequences are so severe.

When I was a newspaper reporter at the *Daily Herald* in suburban Chicago, my best work always came under the most excruciating deadlines.

I'll never forget one story I wrote about a village board meeting. The issue involved a controversial hospital expansion. Hospital officials tried to obtain a necessary permit over the objections of some residents of the village. Vocal opponents feared the mammoth project would damage the ambiance of their rural community.

One night, 200 people packed a room at the village hall that had a maximum capacity of 50. I was 22 years old at the time and had just begun my journalism career. I had a 9:30 p.m. deadline, but the issue was not resolved until 10 p.m. As I anxiously waited for the board to render a ruling, which ultimately went in favor of expansion, I envisioned in my mind how I would write one of three stories: approval, denial or a tabling of the issue with no decision.

When approval finally came, I ran to the mayor and asked him to comment. I found an opponent and asked her to comment. I hurriedly reviewed the architectural drawings to formulate a picture in my mind. I found the nearest phone and called my editor.

"All right, go," my editor, Rich, instructed.

"Go? What do you mean 'go?'" I replied.

"Read me the story," he said.

"I don't have the story. I need time to write it," I answered.

"Todd, this is the real world. We don't have time. Write the story right now in your mind," he ordered. Ten seconds of silence passed. "You ready? Okay. Go."

I took a deep breath, closed my eyes, and wrote the story in my head. Five minutes later, I had compiled 500 words without ever lifting a pen. The next day the story appeared exactly as it was written. There was not one editing change. It was my best work.

"We should do this. We should do that. Until our shoulds become musts, we should all over ourselves."

Anthony Robbins

Make personal and professional goals

Enjoying what you do is important. Enjoying what you do because it enables you lead the life you want is even more important. For instance, it will be much easier to make 100 cold calls if those 100 cold calls are necessary to achieve the income needed to achieve your goal – a Lexus. Or perhaps your goal is to stay physically fit. Staying fit will result in a greater alertness, less irritability and make you more productive in your job … which will enable you to make those 100 cold calls to achieve that income to buy that Lexus. It's a never-ending circle – in a good way. If you asked former NBA star Michael Jordan at the height of his career if he enjoyed lifting weights, he might have had to think about it. But because improving his overall fitness enabled him to be the best of the best, rarely would he miss a workout.

To set personal and professional goals, think backwards. Let's say you want to buy that Lexus. To do so, you need $65,000. To have $65,000, you need $65,000 in commissions. To make $65,000 in commissions, you need to hit 150% of quota on a regular basis. (There are companies, by the way, where the commissions are this exorbitant. Hopefully, you work at one).

See your goals

Computers and hand-written notes help, but who can get really excited about a computer screen or a piece of paper? Find something tangible to represent your goal. Utilize something you can touch and feel.

When I first became a sales manager, I had each of my sales reps write down their professional and personal goals. When the holiday season came around, I made their dreams a reality. I enabled them to see their goals.

For the rep who wanted to earn the money to buy a Porsche in one year, I bought a Porsche. For the rep who wanted a trip to France, I bought a trip to France. For the rep who wanted a camcorder, I bought a camcorder.

The Porsche was a die-cast model Porsche. The trip to France was a puzzle of the Eiffel Tower. The camcorder was a key chain of a ViewMaster. (Remember that toy we played with as kids? You looked into small binoculars to see cartoon photos.) Was it corny? Perhaps. But right up to the day I left, each rep had my gift proudly displayed on their desks.

Determine the goal you want most and figure out how to visualize it. Buy the toy, put the photo on the wall or create a miniature version.

See it. Believe it. Do it.

Celebrate your goals upon accomplishment

Too often, people let life pass them by. They try hard to achieve something, but when they do, they ask, "Is this all there is?" That's because they never take a moment to enjoy how monumental their achievements are.

When you accomplish what you set out to do, be proud. Celebrate your success. Remind yourself that you accomplished your goal. The blood, the sweat and the tears were worth it. If you won an award, post the plaque. If you received that $50,000 commission check, frame it. (Cash it first!) Narcissism is acceptable in celebrating success situations. Whoever gave you those prizes thought highly of you. Think highly of yourself.

Brag to yourself. Take your significant other out to dinner. Buy a nice gift. Spoil yourself. You earned it.

When you enjoy success again, you will want to repeat the feeling. Make it memorable.

"Obstacles are those frightful things you see when you take your eyes off your goals."

Henry Ford

SETTING GOALS EXERCISE:

Take a sheet of paper and list your goals based on the criteria we just discussed. Do the following:

- Make two columns – Personal Goals and Professional Goals.

- List under each column a timeframe: 1 month, 6 months, 1 year and 5 years.

- Under each timeframe list the numbers 1-5.

- There will be 40 items total.

- Write down your goals.

The next page is an example of this goal setting exercise.

My Goals

Personal	Professional

1-Month Goals

Personal	Professional
1. Run 10 k race in under 45 minutes	2 new customers
2. Visit family in Michigan for weekend	Attend 1 networking event
3. Finish *How to Win Friends*	Run 20 new appointments
4. Sleep by 11 p.m., wake up by 7 a.m.	Complete marketing materials
5. Breakfast/lunch, cereal, fruit	Send out first newsletter

6-Month Goals

Personal	Professional
1. Captain softball team into playoffs	Obtain monthly quota
2. Weigh 200	Two months at 150% quota
3. Go to Super Bowl	Attend quarterly Pres. Club
4. Buy 2-bedroom condo for $200,000	Receive 10 referrals per month
5. Take fencing classes	Run 8 new appointments/week

1-Year Goals

Personal	Professional
1. Be extra in movie	$100,000 in income
2. Freelance article for *Selling Power*	$25,000 commission for 1 month
3. Get married	Attend T. Robbins *Date w/Destiny*
4. Buy $25,000 new Honda	Sell 25 new clients
5. Take 1 week trip to Hawaii	Promoted to sales manager

5-Year Goals

Personal	Professional
1. Have 1 child, #2 on the way	Vice President of Sales
2. Own 5-bedroom house in Deerfield	$150,000 base, $50,000 bonuses
3. Host Passover at my house	Manage 50 salespeople, 5 mgrs.
5. Safari Trip in Africa with wife	Have $50,000 in stock
6. Have season tickets to Chicago Bulls	Quoted in national magazine as sales expert

Set your list of goals in a safe place for now. We will reference it throughout this book. You will reference it throughout your life.

Let's recap what we've learned about goals.

1. Write goals down and post them.

2. Make goals measurable.

3. Set deadlines for goals.

4. Make personal and professional goals.

5. Visualize your goals.

6. Celebrate your goals upon accomplishment.

Your professional goals must be structured the same as personal goals – measurable, written and with deadlines. Only if we accomplish our professional goals can we obtain our personal goals.

CHAPTER 2

Schedule

Time Management: A plan to execute your plan to achieve your goals

Preparation and planning prevent poor performance.

Top salespeople don't let prospects and customers fit them into their schedules. They are proactive. Top salespeople fit prospects and customers into *their* schedules.

Since a typical day for a salesperson includes a variety of activities, it's important to manage your time wisely. In any given week, your responsibilities may include running appointments, writing proposals, sending follow-up letters, attending internal meetings (such as one-on-ones with sales managers) and prospecting.

Although tasks that do not involve client contact (such as writing proposals) can be easily done after hours, work-life balance is important. Salespeople should not live and breathe work. The key to fitting essential tasks into regular work days is scheduling.

"Time management" is like writing an individual business plan. Outside factors may alter the plan, but it's critical there be a foundation on which to operate. This foundation will vary from rep to rep.

In this chapter, we will present the playbook for managing your time:

1. Recognize tasks you do each week.

2. Expect Excellence!

3. Create your *must* work week.

4. Commit to your *must* work week.

Recognize tasks you do each week

Have you ever had a day where you worked hard but had nothing to show for it? Have you ever had one of those days where you felt you did absolutely nothing, but somehow eight hours passed and it was time to go home?

What do you really do every day? What do you really do every week? How much time do you really spend working? How much time do you spend working toward those goals you just defined?

Until you know the problem, you can't fix it. Until you know the formula for success, you can't repeat it.

Let's jump right into an exercise.

WEEKLY TASKS I DO EXERCISE:

- Take out a sheet of paper and label it *"Weekly Tasks I Do."*

- Write the numbers 1-25.

- List the tasks you do every week. Do this in two phases.
  1. Rely on your memory. What tasks do you regularly do?
  2. Monitor your tasks over the next week. Add items when necessary.

Before we begin, let's establish some ground rules.

- This is not a list of what you *want* to do. This is what you actually *do*.

- Be honest. Honesty drives this exercise. Write down everything that occupies your time. Our goal is effective time management ... not self-recrimination.

- List at least 25 tasks, but no more than 50.

Share this list with colleagues and your manager to see if you left anything out.

Let's see how you did. Compare your list with the one on the following page. While certain tasks will vary depending on industries, salespeople have things in common across the board. If some tasks are not applicable to what you do, omit them. Just be sure you think hard about each item before crossing it off the list.

You may not understand many of the tasks on the following page at this point. That's okay. We will delve into them one by one in later chapters. This list will give us the basis to build a foundation.

Sales is like life: How much can I accomplish in how much time to achieve how much I want?

50 Tasks I Do Each Week

Prospecting

1. Surf the internet for competitor/prospect/customer information
2. Door knock (in-person cold calls)
3. Follow-up phone calls to door knocking
4. First-time telemarketing phone calls (Yellow Pages, etc.)
5. Follow-up phone calls to telemarketing calls
6. Phone conversations to acquire referrals
7. Phone calls to these referrals
8. Referrals given to you via e-mail introduction
9. Return e-mail to referral e-mails
10. Return prospects' phone calls
11. Send out info after phone conversation to get appointment
12. Send out info after first conversation prior to first appointment
13. Send out info after phone conversation to uninterested prospect – "Keep me in files"
14. Send out intro letter/referral e-mail when can't reach via phone

Appointments

15. Send out thank you letter after the first meeting (follow-up meeting scheduled)
16. Send out agenda prior to the first meeting
17. Run first appointment
18. Send out thank you letter with no interest after first meeting
19. Send out agenda prior to second meeting
20. Run second appointment (deliver proposal/demonstration)
21. Closing appointment
22. Send out agenda prior to phone meeting
23. Run phone appointment

Networking

24. Send referral e-mail – you give lead to someone else
25. Leave voice mail for networking opportunity
26. Networking phone conversation
27. Networking lunch to swap leads

50 Tasks I Do Each Week (cont.)

Customer Issues

28. Phone calls to current customers for status
29. E-mails to current customers for status
30. Return phone calls for current customer issues
31. Return e-mail for current customer issues
32. Thank you letters to customers

Internal Office Work

33. Check work voice mail
34. Dial information (411)
35. Check personal e-mail on the internet
36. Check personal phone calls at home
37. Make personal phone calls
38. Read internal junk e-mail
39. Respond to internal junk e-mail
40. Internal manager reports
41. Internal paperwork for orders
42. Respond to internal paperwork issues
43. Thank you e-mail to colleagues/support people for job well done

Internal Meetings

44. Sales Manager weekly meetings
45. Sales Manager one-on-ones
46. Internal conference calls/training

Research

47. Write proposals
48. Read e-mailed newsletters/newspapers
49. Assemble media kits
50. Socialize

Were the results of this exercise enlightening? Shocking? Did you expect to see what you recorded?

Take a hard look at your list. Ask yourself the following:

- How much time was spent prospecting?
- How much time was spent conducting appointments?
- How much time did you spend checking voice mail?
- How much time did you spend surfing the internet during working hours doing "research?"
- How much time did you spend making personal calls?
- How many times did you log on and log back off to log back on again to check e-mail?
- How much time did you spend during work hours doing paperwork?
- How much time did you spend doing paperwork and proposals during office hours – client contact time – that could have been done after hours?
- How much time did you spend in the car?
- Did you find yourself driving 50 miles between appointments, wasting valuable time?
- Were your appointments near one another?
- How many e-mail conversations did you have with internal colleagues rather than picking up the phone to have a brief live conversation to resolve an issue?

Our intent is not to break down your confidence. This is a reality check. There were probably quite a few tasks you didn't notice you did – things you take for granted, such as checking voice mail or even socializing.

Sales is a tough job in its own right. Actually, the salesperson who is a devoted workaholic often does more damage than good. Playing and having fun in an office situation are okay.

Working hard is important. But working smart is more important.

The list you just created is critical because it determines your individual formula for success. If you socialize three hours a week and are at 200% of quota regularly, this play time is part of your formula for success. Great salespeople and managers recognize that sales formulas go beyond how many appointments were run or how many phone calls were made.

We are now creating the playbook we discussed earlier.

Expect Excellence!

Time management is different than goal-setting because goal-setting suggests a long-term orientation. Time management is here and now. While long-term goals are essential, so are short-term objectives.

We have established what we want to accomplish in one month, six months, one year and five years. Now, what do we need to accomplish on a daily, weekly and monthly basis to accomplish our goals? What does it take to achieve our quotas? What is your quota?

In almost every situation, there are two kinds of quotas; what your company mandates and your own.

"The outstanding leaders of every age are those who set up their own quotas and constantly exceed them."
Thomas J. Watson, former chairman of IBM

If you work for a large corporation, your company will probably help you determine this monthly target. Your manager may meet with you weekly to ensure you have run a certain number of appointments, delivered a certain number of proposals and phoned a certain number of prospects.

If you are self-employed, you have a tougher challenge because, while you answer to no one in theory, the challenge is that you actually answer to the most important person of all –

yourself. Even in the corporate environment, your real account-ability is to yourself.

Focus on what you do. To accomplish those monumental long-term goals based on the tasks you have outlined, compile weekly business goals. These goals will include prospecting phone calls, scheduled appointments, completed appointments, etc.

There is a concept in sales known as the 1/3, 1/3, 1/3 rule. This rule is based on the theory that you have 99 potential sales opportunities. The top 33 will close no matter what. It does not matter if you have no sales skills or if you are selling to a 10-year-old kid. This sale is a sure thing. Everything fits. This is the right time and right place opportunity salespeople treasure. This includes prospects contacting you or signing up your boss's friend.

The bottom 33 opportunities are the exact opposite: No one could sell these accounts. You could have the selling skills of Zig Ziglar. It would not matter. These opportunities often have hidden "deal-breakers" (we will explain this concept later in greater detail). For example, the prospect may be bound to a 10-year contract with a $1 million penalty for breaking an agreement. Or maybe the prospect uses the services of their boss's best friend. Too many times salespeople spend days trying to close this bottom third. What they should be doing is focusing on the middle 33.

In 99 opportunities, 1/3 will close for sure, 1/3 won't close for sure. It's the middle 1/3 we call sales.

One rep may need to call 100 companies to schedule five appointments, while another rep may only need to call 10 to schedule the same five appointments. One rep may need five appointments to close a deal, while another rep may need two appointments. The key is recognizing what you need.

What's your process?

"EXPECT EXCELLENCE!" EXERCISE

- Take a sheet of paper. Label it *"Expect Excellence!"*

- Write a numeric quantity for each task you want to accomplish based on the previous exercise *"Tasks I Do."*

- At the minimum, this list will include the following:
  - Deals sold
  - Scheduled appointments
  - Completed appointments
  - Networking appointments
  - First time phone calls
  - Follow-up phone calls
  - E-mail marketing contacts

Compare your list to the sample telecommunications salesperson list on the next page.

Until you expect the best, you can never achieve the best.

Expect Excellence!
(Example: Telecommunications Sales)

Recommended
> *Based on monthly sales quota: $4,000 in new business*
> *200% is the goal – $8,000*

Weekly Objectives
1 deal/week ($2,000 x 4=$8,000)

- __7__ first appointments
- __2__ second appointments (proposal presentation)
- __1__ closing appointment
- __2__ phone appointments
- __2__ networking appointments
- __1__ nightly networking event/two weeks
- __2__ referrals given via e-mail to someone
- __10__ scheduled appointments made that week (2/day)

- __30__ in-person cold calls
- __30__ blind cold telemarketing calls
- __20__ networking first calls (contact from past life)
- __30__ follow-up phone calls (can't reach)

- __10__ e-mail first contacts (can't reach via phone)
- __6__ e-mail thanks with concrete next appointment

> *"What really counts is what we learn after we know it all."*
>
> John Wooden, former coach of UCLA collegiate basketball who won 10 national championships

In *50 Tasks I Do Each Week Exercise,* you identified your regular activities. The *Establish Excellence Exercise* provided insight about the activities you perform that further your sales.

Now we will combine the two exercises in the *What I Must Do in the Future Exercise.* We will create a dream schedule that realistically groups the activities you currently do in a way that allows you to be "excellent" and to perform more efficiently.

In essence you will be creating a business plan.

WHAT I *MUST* DO IN THE FUTURE EXERCISE

- Take out five sheets of paper and label each *"What I Must Do Weekly Schedule."*

- Under *"Weekly Schedule"* label each page with a day: Monday, Tuesday, Wednesday, Thursday and Friday.

- Under the day, list a work day of 8:00-5:30. For the sake of this exercise, we will categorize this as a typical work day. If yours is more or less, alter the times accordingly. Allocate approximate one hour time slots (although certain alterations need to be made). Here's a suggested schedule:

     8 - 8:30 a.m.
     8:30 - 9:30 a.m.
     9:30 - 10:30 a.m.
     10:30 -12:00 p.m.
     12 - 1 p.m.
     1 - 2 p.m.
     2 - 3 p.m.
     3 - 4 p.m.
     4 - 5 p.m.
     5 - 5:30 p.m.

- Take your *Tasks I Do Each Week* and schedule those items on the above 5-day agenda, using the *Expect Excellence!* sheets as a barometer for what you want to accomplish.

- Create a "Dream" schedule, inserting critical tasks into allocated time slots. Include quantities, time and other specifics when appropriate.

Compare your schedule to the sample schedule on page 28.

When making prospecting phone calls, include how many calls you will make in each time bracket. If critical research for a proposal needs to be done during working hours, you obviously can't include a quantity ... but do include a timeframe. Also, when referencing appointments, include the drive time between destinations.

This dream schedule will fluctuate – probably on a regular basis. The idea is to create your individual playbook for success. If salespeople did have total control over every aspect of their day, what would they do? You'd be amazed at how many would let the day slip by. Top salespeople never do.

In creating your dream schedule, follow these rules to maximize effectiveness:

Cluster/Use repetition

In sales, as in life, good organization is based on the same tasks being performed at the same time, on the same day.

The law of physics says that motion creates motion. Momentum is everything.

Do you exercise? Think about your routines or those of someone you know. Ask them when they exercise. Ask them what day and what time. True fitness people always have strict schedules. They have a process. If they miss even one day, they go into a form of withdrawal. That's because they trust the routine. It's what they know.

Have you ever woken up and not gotten out of bed? You feel uncomfortable. Getting up is part of your routine.

For your sales playbook, create "appointment days," "prospecting days," etc. It's a fact that one of the main reasons businesses fail is they lack focus. Simplify the process so that you can focus on fewer items at a time. The way to do this is to schedule certain tasks on certain days. Know when your appointments will occur before they occur. Some salespeople worry that having strict guidelines will be too "pushy" when it comes to working with prospects and customers. It's quite the opposite. Nothing is worse than dealing with an unsure salesperson – one who does not know how to ask for an appointment or ask for a deal.

Don't be a "star" salesperson. In sales, a "star" salesperson is not the top sales rep. On the contrary, the star is the person with the worst time management skills. A star salesperson is a rep who goes into the office at 8 a.m., drives one hour north to the first appointment, heads back two hours south to the second appointment, then heads three hours east to the third appointment. If you draw a map of the route of the salesperson on a typical day, the point of his destinations resemble a star. Plan your appointments so they are near each other. Group your office activities, your meeting locations and your door knocking in the same locations.

People like to do business with busy, successful people. It's the same reason everyone wants to be friends with the popular kid in school. Subconsciously, they like someone just because others like that person. Sales is no different.

Do items that do not involve client contact off hours

Clients and prospects – and other non-salespeople – generally can only be reached between 8 a.m. and 5 p.m. Sometimes reaching business people during these hours can be difficult with everyone's busy schedule. While tasks such as writing proposals and doing expenses are necessary parts of your job, *you* control when these items will be conducted. There will be times when you may have to work on proposals during the day because you need internal help from non-salespeople, but try to minimize these times. Take advantage of prime time hours to call clients and prospects. They are the ones who pay you.

- Set aside 15 minutes before work every day to list goals for the day. Save 15 minutes at the end of the day to list goals for the next day.

- Eat breakfast and lunch every day.

  Some people consider it a badge of honor to skip breakfast or lunch. Why? This results in a lack of energy and productivity. The body needs physical nourishment. Selling is a tough job physically and emotionally.

  Eat. These meals affect your productivity the entire work day.

- E-mail off line.

  Although most non-money making tasks should be done after hours, exceptions must be made. E-mail is one of those exceptions.

  E-mail is a tremendous resource. But do not get engaged in "conversations" on a computer screen.

Salespeople should only use e-mail as a form of marketing, accountability and clarification – not communication.

By e-mailing offline, you will accomplish more in less time. Once in "e-mail mode," you can accomplish all your work without the distractions of the beep begging you to stop what you are doing and respond. Once you are done creating all your e-mails offline, connect online and send your mail.

No one expects an immediate response to e-mail. If you lived strictly "on" your computer, you would never run appointments and never meet with clients and prospects. If you lived on the computer, you would not be in sales.

It is acceptable to reply to e-mail one full day later.

Sample Must Work Week
(Example: Telecommunications Sales)

Mondays

7:45 a.m.	Arrive at work/Write Daily Goals
8 a.m.	Check e-mail/respond to e-mail
8:30-9:30 a.m.	Weekly Sales Meeting?
9:30 - 10:30 a.m	E-mail agendas (PALS - will be discussed in upcoming chapters) for Tuesday meetings
10:30 - 12 p.m.	E-mail thank you letters/proposals
12 p.m.-1 p.m.	Lunch
1 -1:30 p.m.	Phone appointment 1
2 - 2:30 p.m.	Phone appointment 2
2:30 - 4:30 p.m.	20 networking first calls
4:30 - 5:15 p.m.	Proposal work
5:15 - 5:30 p.m.	Respond to e-mail/List To Do Goals for tomorrow

Tuesdays

7:45 a.m.	Arrive at work/Write Daily Goals
8 a.m.	Check e-mail/respond to e-mail/prepare for appointments
8:30 - 9:30 a.m.	Appointment 1
10 - 11 a.m.	Appointment 2
11:30 - 1 p.m.	Appointment 3
1 - 2 p.m.	Lunch
2:30- 3:30 p.m.	Appointment 4
4 - 5 p.m.	Appointment 5
5 - 5:30	Respond to e-mail/List To Do Goals for tomorrow

Sample Must Work Week (cont.)

Wednesdays

7:45 a.m.	Arrive at work/Write Daily Goals
8 -8:30 a.m.	Check e-mail/respond to e-mail
8:30 - 12:30 p.m.	First calls (blind telemarketing) – _30_
12 - 1 p.m.	Go back online/send e-mails/ lunch (network appointment)
1:30 - 5:30 p.m.	Follow-up Calls (couldn't reach before) – _30_
5:30 - 6:00 p.m.	Respond to e-mail/List To Do Goals for tomorrow

Thursdays

7:45 a.m.	Arrive at work/Write Daily Goals
8 - 8:30 a.m.	Check e-mail/respond to e-mail
8:30 - 9:30 a.m.	Appointment 6
10 - 11 a.m.	Appointment 7
11:30 -1 p.m.	Appointment 8
1 - 2 p.m.	Lunch
2:30- 3:30 p.m.	Appointment 9
4 - 5 p.m.	Appointment 10
5 - 5:30 p.m.	Respond to e-mail/List To Do Goals for tomorrow

Fridays

7:45 a.m.	Arrive at work/Write Daily Goals
8 - 8:30 a.m.	Check e-mail/respond to e-mail
8:30 - 9:30 a.m.	Thank you letters from meetings
9:30 -12 p.m.	In-person cold calls – _20_
12 -1 p.m.	Lunch
1 - 2:30 p.m.	In-person cold calls – _10_
2:30 - 5 p.m.	10 e-mail first contacts; 13 e-mail thank you for meetings

Commit to your *must* work week

You've created your schedule. How does it look? Are you excited? Does it provide structure? Did you follow all the proper criteria? You now have your roadmap to success! But for this schedule to work, you need to commit to it. Don't treat this as a *possible* schedule. Treat this as your schedule.

If you say that Wednesdays are prospecting days, then prospect on Wednesdays. If your schedule indicates you will make 50 calls on this day, then make 50 calls. Don't schedule appointments. If Monday is an office day and afternoons are when you slotted sending e-mails, send e-mails (off line) at the appointed time. Try hard to not let your manager force a meeting. (Good managers should not be calling meetings on a moment's notice anyway.) Don't return phone calls during this time.

If you slot appointments on Tuesdays and Thursdays at designated times, but then you don't have appointments on these days, you *should* feel bad. Make yourself feel bad enough so that you are determined to not let that happen again!

Fill up your schedule to fit the week. Don't fill up your week to fit the schedule.

When was the last time your doctor moved his schedule around for you, the patient? Aren't you the one paying the bill? Why should sales be any different? Who's to say a salesperson is less important than a doctor? Never view prospects as doing you a favor by meeting with you. Instead recognize how lucky they are to have access to your expertise.

Selling is the ability to influence others in an effort to achieve a desired result that is mutually beneficial to enhance one another's lives.

When you create a schedule and you are asking prospects for appointments, pick the time. Tell prospects when you are available; don't ask when they are available. If a prospect wants to meet on your "telemarketing" day, tell the prospect you are busy and pick a date and time that works for you.

Emergencies, such as customer service issues, will surface. Some issues will need to be addressed on the spot and schedules will need to be altered. Don't become so tied to your schedule that there is no flexibility. But do work at being able to recognize what really is an emergency versus situations when you are catering unnecessarily to someone else's needs at the expense of your own.

Some sales reps lean on the customer emergency issue as a crutch. Don't fall into that trap.

Ask yourself this question every time you are asked to readjust your schedule: "If you were in front of a prospect closing a deal, if the prospect was signing the agreement then and there, would you leave the meeting? Would you answer the phone? Would you respond to e-mail?" If the answer is no, because what you are doing at that moment is "important," then your schedule should not be altered.

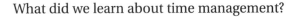
What did we learn about time management?

1. Recognize tasks you do each week.
2. Expect Excellence!
3. Create your *must* work week.
4. Commit to your *must* work week.

The best sales reps value their own time –
more than the customer's.

CHAPTER 3

State Initial Benefit

Initial Benefit Statement: An explanation of what you are offering, what it means and why anyone should care – in the exact opposite order

Put yourself in the position of prospects. Ask yourself what they ask themselves: "What's in it for me?"

Why should someone consider buying your product? Why should they take the time to hear you out, let alone meet with you? What are you offering? What makes it so good?

If you don't believe in your product or your services, no one else will. But believing in what you offer goes beyond having a good mental mindset. Being able to articulate in a clear, concise manner is essential to succeeding in sales.

You must be able to state your initial benefit as a universal message. Having a "scripted" commercial explaining how you can help others from the onset is critical to your success. You will customize it to individual situations since each client is different, but you need to have a universal message you can explain easily.

If you door knock, state your initial benefit to receptionists and secretaries. Why else should they help you get in the door to speak with the person in charge? If you are at a networking event, your initial benefit statement should intrigue others so they will chat with you rather than move on to the next attendee.

If you were from Publisher's Clearing House and your job was to visit businesses to give them checks for $1 million, do you think top company executives would stop what they are doing to speak with you for a moment? It would depend on what you say. If you say to the first person you meet "I'd like to speak to So-and-So" without identifying who you were and your purpose, it would be hard to get an audience with a top executive.

Imagine this conversation. (But first let's change the name from Publisher's Clearing House to ABC Company since most people would recognize the Publisher's Clearing House name. Remember, our job is still to give away $1 million dollars.)

Salesperson:	"I'd like to see the president of the company."
Receptionist:	"He's busy now. What is this regarding? Perhaps I can help you."
Salesperson:	"No, I don't think so. It's important. I'm from ABC Company."
Receptionist:	"What's this regarding?"
Salesperson:	"Please just tell him I'm here."
Receptionist:	"He's busy. Why don't you leave your name and number?"

Now let's make one small change in this conversation. What if the salesperson says, "I'm stopping by to give him $1 million that he has won"? Wouldn't the receptionist immediately find the president?

In this chapter, we will present the playbook for stating the initial benefit:

1. What are the *features* of your company?

2. What are the *advantages* of your company?

3. What are the *benefits* of your company?

4. Who is your ideal customer?

5. State your initial benefit – in writing.

6. Know when and how to use your Initial Benefit Statement.

What are the *features* of your company?

Before you can properly state your initial benefit, identify what you have in your arsenal. Features are the services and products you actually provide. If you sell phone service, features include long distance lines, calling cards, toll-free numbers and the actual phone bill (whether it is sent via paper or electronically). Features also include amenities such as 24-hour customer service. If you sell copiers or other tangible equipment, the various models, warranties and leasing options are features.

Specifics about your company also are categorized as features. If your company is 50 years old and has 100 employees with 20 customer service people, being 50 years old, having 100 employees and 20 customer service people are all features. When customers buy your services, these are features they will receive.

What are the features of *your* product?

WHAT I OFFER EXERCISE

- Take a sheet of paper and label it *"What I Offer."*

- Underneath the *"What I Offer"* write *"Features."*

- List 20 features of your physical product and service.

- This list should include at least 5 features of your company.

- The remaining 15 may be features of the products you sell.

Compare your list to the following TBN Sales Solutions example.

What I Offer
Example: TBN Sales Solutions

Features

1. Todd Natenberg, President, TBN Sales Solutions
   - 10 years sales experience/management/training
   - Former journalist
   - Sold telecommunications, copiers, shoes
   - Book author
   - Adventurer – including two-month sabbatical in Israel, hang gliding, scuba diving, parasailing
   - Freelance articles to various sales publications
2. Author of the book *"I just got a job in sales. Now what?"*
3. DiSC Personality Profile provider
4. *Skyrocketing Sales Solutions!* electronic newsletter
5. Advertisement for clients in newsletter
6. Advertisement for clients on www.toddnatenberg.com web site
7. Customized corporate sales training workshops
8. 1/2 day to 1 week programs
9. Customized 12-week individual sales coaching – one hour on the phone per week
10. One hour per week one-on-one phone training
11. Public teleseminar workshops
12. Public workshops
13. Workbook handouts for corporate sales training workshops
14. Electronic handouts for individual sales coaching
15. Written role plays
16. Verbal evaluation of sales force
17. Written evaluation of sales force/recommendations
18. Month to month programs – pay as you go
19. Package deals to reduce cost
20. Multiple clients with proven results

What are the *advantages* of your company?

Now that you know what you offer, determine why it is better than what the competition offers – including why it is better than what the prospect already has.

This is called the advantage. No matter what the service or product, sales involves asking individuals to change. Somehow, some way, what you are offering will make someone else's life better – but different, too. This could mean you are providing a new service the prospect does not have, or it could be that you are replacing an existing service. Either way, if you can't explain why what you are offering is better than what they currently have, they won't purchase.

A critical difference between advantages and benefits is that an advantage is the *salesperson's* interpretation of why a feature is better. The advantage is a universal application caused by change. A benefit is tailored to the individual prospect. It is customized.

In the world of phone service, a feature of one company might be online phone billing. The advantage is that with online billing, the customer won't have to mail phone bills. Because the customer won't have to mail phone bills, the situation improves. It is better than the current situation. The difficulty is that perhaps the customer *wants* to mail phone bills. It's only an advantage because the salesperson defines it as an advantage.

Let's use the payroll industry as another example. If one payroll company offers an assigned account manager to its customers, the feature is the assigned account manager. The advantage is that the customer will have one point of contact – a situation that does not currently exist. A competing payroll company may not offer an assigned account manager. Having the assigned account manager is not the advantage. Having one point of contact is the advantage.

What are *your* company's and products' advantages?

WHY MY PRODUCT IS BETTER EXERCISE

- Take a sheet of paper and label it *"Why My Product is Better."*

- Underneath the *"Why My Product is Better"* write *"Advantages."*

- Return to your features list.

- Write advantages of each of the 15 features of the product.

- Write advantages of each of the 5 features of the company.

The #1 advantage of your #1 feature should always be you. Be sure you emphasize that your years of industry experience mean that you have an understanding that others might not possess. If you have minimal industry experience, be sure to mention that because you are greener, you care more and are more eager to learn. Because you have fewer customers, those you do have get more attention.

What about other advantages? How do they separate you from your competition? See the following page for another example.

Why My Product is Better

Example: TBN Sales Solutions

Advantages

1. Diverse background provides fresh perspective on sales training
2. Sales book offers credibility, proven methodologies in the public domain
3. DiSC, the foundation for the team-building workshop, provides customized sales training based on individual needs
4. Newsletter offers credibility, proven methodologies in the public domain
5. Client ads in newsletter increase exposure for additional business
6. Client ads on web site increase exposure for additional business
7. Customized corporate sales training enables clients to have training catered to their needs
8. 1/2 day to 1 week programs offers multiple services for unique needs
9. 12-week individual sales coaching offers one-on-one attention
10. One hour per week allows quick hits training for immediate impact
11. Teleseminar offers multiple services for unique needs and is cost-effective
12. Public workshops offer reduced cost for diverse classroom participants
13. Workbook handouts enable "take aways" for concrete strategies
14. Electronic handouts enable easy "cut and paste" features for templates
15. Written role plays allow fast translation of theory into practices
16. Verbal evaluation of sales force provides outside perspective to improve
17. Written evaluation allows "take aways" for concrete strategies
18. Pay as you go allows a payment plan that fits your budget
19. Package deals reduce costs
20. Multiple clients offer credibility with proven impact

What are the *benefits* of your company?

Why should prospects care what you are offering? What's in it for them? What impact will your offer have on their business?

A *benefit* is how your product will help your customers. It's a "translation" of the features and advantages to fit the individual prospect. Knowing and being able to verbalize benefits of your product separates you from your competition. Knowing benefits makes you a professional ... not just another salesperson. It gives you the ability to close those 33 opportunities that we discussed earlier.

For instance, a *feature* that TBN Sales Solutions offers is this book, *"I just got a job in sales. Now what?"* The *advantage* is that it provides written methodologies from the perspective of a former sales manager and trainer who still sells on a daily basis. Because of this perspective, readers receive a firsthand account from someone in the trenches with them. Being in the trenches and still selling are advantages of Todd Natenberg. The *benefit* is that these methodologies – if executed properly – will skyrocket salespeoples' commissions. "Skyrocketing commissions" is why you should care.

The best way to recognize benefits is to insert the words "which is a good thing because this means you will now be able to ..."

The benefits of what you offer will normally fall into four categories. The specific description of your benefits is up to you, but, traditionally, benefits:

- Increase revenue and profitability

- Increase efficiency

- Reduce costs and expenditures

- Impact the bottom line

As you will see on the following page, at TBN Sales Solutions we like to relate these benefits to "skyrocketing your sales."

WHY THEY SHOULD CARE EXERCISE

- Take a sheet of paper and label it *"Why They Should Care."*

- Underneath *"Why They Should Care,"* write *"Benefits."*

- Write 20 benefits.

Compare your list to the following example.

Why They Should Care

Example: TBN Sales Solutions

("which is a good thing because this means you will now be able to.....")

Benefits

1. Fresh perspective means you will now be able to get the latest up-to-date information to skyrocket your sales

2. Credibility and proven methodologies means you will now be able to use the most effective tools today to skyrocket your sales

3. Customized sales training means you will be able to utilize techniques based on your individual skillset to skyrocket your sales

4. Newsletter that offers credibility and proven methodologies means you will now be able to use the most effective tools today to skyrocket your sales

5. Client ads in newsletter increase exposure for additional business which means you will now be able to skyrocket your sales

6. Client ads on website increase exposure for additional business which means you will now be able to skyrocket your sales

7. Training catered to your needs means you will have individual needs addressed to skyrocket your sales

8. Various options of 1/2 day to 1 week means all departments can benefit from ongoing training in various areas to skyrocket sales

9. One on one attention means you will have individual needs addressed to skyrocket your sales.

10. Quick hits training for immediate impact means you will be able to hit the ground running to skyrocket your sales

(continued on next page)

Why They Should Care (cont.)

11. Multiple services for unique needs means the cost-effective program will make it affordable to skyrocket your sales

12. Public workshops offer reduced cost for diverse participants which means you will be able to participate – even with economic limitations – in order to skyrocket your sales

13. Takeaways enable you to apply what is learned after the training has ended to skyrocket your sales

14. "Cut and Paste" features reduce follow-up sales time which means you will be able to skyrocket your sales

15. Translating theory into practice allows you to hit ground running to skyrocket sales

16. Gaining an outside perspective means you will be able to increase your knowledge base to separate you from the rest to skyrocket your sales

17. Written evaluation allows "take aways" for concrete strategies providing more ways to skyrocket your sales

18. Plans to fit your budget means training is available when needed so you can afford to skyrocket your sales

19. Reduced costs mean more training to skyrocket your sales

20. Multiple clients mean you are working with someone who has a good perspective to skyrocket your sales

Who is your ideal customer?

While most salespeople know what they are selling, why it's better and why others should care, they often fail to identify their customers. Everyone is not a prospect. For instance, TBN Sales Solutions does not look to train lawyers on sales skills. Of course we will train anyone who wants to improve their sales skills, but lawyers are not our target.

Who's *your* target? Remember, this is your "initial benefit statement." In defining your ideal client, ask yourself the following questions.

Questions to ask defining an ideal client

- Who are you selling to?
- Who would sign on the dotted line?
- What kind of services are already in place?
- What industry?
- How many employees?
- What is their annual revenue?
- Who is the current provider of services you offer?
- Does the company have your services from another provider? Is this to your advantage?
- Who is the decision-maker? Is it the CEO, CFO or Controller ... or someone else?
- What are the personality traits of your typical decision-maker?
- Where are they located? What city? What state?
- Do they have conservative or liberal buying habits?
- Are they at one location or many locations?
- Are they computer savvy?
- Are they technologically advanced?
- How old is the company?
- Are they a small business? (however you define small)
- Are they a mid-sized business?
- Are they a large business?
- Where are headquarters?
- What is the international presence?
- Are they publicly traded?

WHO I SELL TO EXERCISE

- Take a sheet of paper and label it *"Who do I sell to?"*

- Return to your *Features* list.

- Return to your *Advantages* list.

- Return to your *Benefits* lists.

- Based on these three criteria (and with your boss's help), describe your ideal customer.

Write Initial Benefit Statement

It's time to write your initial benefit statement! The statement should include a synopsis of a few sentences about your features, advantages, benefits and target customer. Traditional sales methods say your statement should be no longer than 20 seconds, but the fact is there's no harm in running slightly longer because sometimes longer is more effective.

In writing your initial benefit statement, look to elicit the "No kidding!" response. This is named in honor of my former editor, Mark Shepherd, at the *Columbia Missourian.* Shep said that when reading the lead of a story (in essence, our initial benefit statement), readers should say, "No kidding!" This proves you have aroused interest.

Before writing your initial benefit statement, let's review the four components:

- Features

- Advantages

- Benefits

- Ideal customer

Here's an example:

> "TBN Sales Solutions increases commissions for salespeople and profits for businesses through customized training, coaching and consulting. By establishing structures and procedures in all facets of the sales process, through classroom workshops and individual sales coaching, we teach reps to control their own destinies, to impact the bottom line."

Do you recognize the features? Are there advantages and benefits? Do you recognize the ideal customer? Did you say, "No kidding!"?

Let's find out. Take the following quiz. An answer key is included for your convenience.

Features-**A**dvantages-**B**enefits QUIZ

"TBN Sales Solutions increases commissions for sales-people and profits for businesses through customized training, coaching and consulting. By establishing structures and procedures in all facets of the sales process, through classroom workshops and individual sales coaching, we teach reps to control their own destinies, thereby impacting the bottom line."

What are the features?

a.

b.

c.

d.

e.

f.

What are the advantages?

a.

What are the benefits?

a.

b.

c.

Who is the ideal customer?

a.

b.

F-A-B Quiz Answers

Features
a. Customized training
b. Customized coaching
c. Customized consulting
d. Establishing structures and procedures
e. Workshops
f. Individual sales coaching

Advantages
a. Control their own destinies

Benefits
a. Increase profits
b. Increase commissions
c. Impact the bottom line

Ideal Customer
a. Salespeople
b. Businesses

Let's examine the Features/Advantages/Benefits questions one at a time.

Features

What does TBN Sales Solutions offer? We offer training, coaching and consulting. What about the term "customized?" Isn't that an advantage ... or even a benefit?

While customized training is better than just "plain" training, it's still a feature. It's a type of training. Customization is not an advantage or benefit. It's the type of training TBN Sales Solutions offers. Some companies offer general training; TBN Sales Solutions offers customized training. Both have their own advantages and benefits.

Likewise, establishing structures and procedures is specific information, but it's still just what TBN does. It's not an advantage. It's how the workshops, the coaching and the consulting are structured.

Advantages

By providing training, coaching and consulting, TBN Sales Solutions "teaches reps to control their own destinies." This makes TBN better than the rest – at least from our perspective! Therefore it becomes an advantage.

Benefits

Increasing commissions, increasing profits and impacting the bottom line are three reasons why the prospects should care. They will help the prospect – if we accomplish what we set out to do.

INITIAL BENEFIT STATEMENT EXERCISE

- Take a sheet of paper and label it *"Initial Benefit Statements."*

- Return to your *Features* exercise.

- Return to your *Advantages* exercise.

- Return to your *Benefits* exercise.

- Write three separate initial benefit statements.

- Pick the best one.

Know when and how to use your Initial Benefit Statement

"Opportunities multiply as they are seized."

Sun Tzu (c.500 - 320 bc)

After creating this terrific initial benefit statement, many salespeople never use it again. When should you state your initial benefit? As they say about voting in Chicago, use your initial benefit statement "early and often."

Use it in your signature (E-mail or written letter)

Any time you send a note to anyone, whether a personal friend or a business associate, add a line about what you do, no matter how long this makes your signature. Most people don't like selling friends. But if you do not alert them to your expertise, you are missing a great opportunity. All e-mail programs have an automatic feature to preset your signature.

Take advantage of signatures. The benefits will be obvious.

Use it when you describe your job to others

Don't be uncomfortable stating your initial benefit when people ask what you do for a living. Be proud of the fact that you do much more than "sell phone service." Take TBN Sales Solutions as an example. What do I do? You could simply say that I own a sales training company. But is that entirely accurate? Does that detail what TBN Sales Solutions is all about? In describing my company that way, I'd actually be cheating others out of learning details describing my true offerings.

Many times people respond to my statement "increase commissions for salespeople ..." with "I'm in sales and I'm having trouble. Maybe you can help me." Another common response is "I have a friend in sales who could use your help." You never know when opportunities will surface.

Use it at networking events

State your initial benefits statement over and over at networking events! If you want to earn business and garner referrals, don't tell people at a networking event *what* you do. Everyone does that. Tell them *why* they should care. It will set you apart from the rest. (More in the Networking chapter.)

Use it in your first encounter with prospects

Your first encounter is usually not with the person who signs on the dotted line. Remember the Publisher's Clearing House example? Give the secretary a reason to find the boss. Besides, you can never be sure in a first encounter that you are talking to the secretary. Perhaps the president of the company is filling in for the receptionist during lunch.

Use it at the start of every sales appointment

Just because you are meeting with a prospect does not mean the prospect remembers what you do. Use the initial benefit statement to remind the prospect not only what you do, but why the two of you are meeting.

Let's recap.

---

1. What are the features of your company?

2. What are the advantages of your company?

3. What are the benefits of your company?

4. Who is your ideal customer?

5. State your initial benefit – in writing.

6. Know when and how to use your Initial Benefit Statement.

Features are what you offer. Advantages are why you are better. Benefits are why they should care. State all three.

CHAPTER 4

Prospect

Prospecting: Uncovering qualified opportunities through various methods in an effort to advance potential clients in the sales process

Whenever I get depressed and think my work is for naught, I think of stonecutters. They spend their lives chipping away at stones without leaving even so much as a dent. Then, one day they tap the stone and the entire object breaks. But what they must remember is were it not for the first five million whacks, the stone never would have broken.

Earn the right to sell. Before you give your sales pitch, the initial benefit statement, establish trust and rapport with your prospects. You may have a great product and a great 30-second initial benefit statement, but if you don't have an interested audience, what you say is a moot point. You only have one chance to make a great impression.

Don't waste it.

Think about how prosecuting attorneys interrogate witnesses or how police officers question suspects. Do they immediately accuse defendants of being guilty? First, they develop rapport. They offer a cup of coffee or a soda (at least according to television and movies). Then they ease into their questioning. They ask non-threatening questions, followed by harder questions, and not until the very end do they come right out and say, "Admit it. Admit it! You did it!! Admit it!!!"

> *"Seek to understand before seeking to be understood."*
> Stephen Covey

This strategy should not be limited to use in sales appointments. From the moment you first contact your prospect, begin creating trust. It does not matter whether you are talking to the true "decision-maker." As we indicated in the last chapter, until you get to know the company, always assume you are speaking with the person in charge.

Recognize that everyone is a decision-maker in their own right. Besides, the people who sign on the dotted line and the people who "claim" they are decision-makers often vary. More than one salesperson has had a prospect answer the "Are you the decision-maker?" question with "Yes ... I just need to run it by So-and-So to approve it."

Never come down to people's levels. Come up to their levels.

In this next chapter, we will present the playbook for prospecting:

1. Prepare.

2. Decide how to prospect.

3. Introduce and humanize.

4. Explain why you selected this particular company.

5. State Initial Benefit.

6. Ask for appointment.

7. Empower.

8. Close for appointment.

Prepare

Effective prospecting is a mindset. You need to understand what you are trying to accomplish, why you want to accomplish it and how you will accomplish it. The best salespeople do not view prospecting as drudgery. They view it as a means to an end.

Everyone and every company are not prospects. They are "suspects." They might *become* a prospect, but not until certain criteria are revealed, such as their timeframe, whether solutions can be provided to meet their needs and whether they have sufficient resources.

Firm date, firm time each week

You have already outlined what days and what times you will prospect. Execute your plan. Remember that these are appointments. They are no different than the appointments you schedule with prospects. Rarely would you cancel an appointment with someone who may buy your service. Treat the time you prospect no differently.

Like the fitness buff who sticks to a daily routine, prospect on the same day at the same time each week. Momentum is everything. Clusters are key. Have prospecting days and prospecting times, much like you will have appointment slots to schedule. Some sales managers may try to fill your prospecting days with other group activities. Try to stick to your schedule. "I have 50 appointments on Wednesday from 8:30 to 5 p.m.," tell them.

"But I thought you were prospecting?" they may ask.

"Exactly. Those are my appointments." (Then show them your schedule from last chapter.)

Leave your desk (Call from a conference room, if you can)

Desks are distractions for even the most organized sales-person, because they remind us of all the things we have to do over a period of time. We are surrounded by temptation. Presentation kits, files, phone numbers, e-mails, voice mail messages and more are all within our reach.

What separates Tiger Woods and Michael Jordan from other great athletes is their ability to focus on tasks at hand – sinking the 20 foot putt or making the game-winning shot. Nothing more. Nothing less.

Forward voice mail/Turn off cell phone/ Don't connect to the internet

Voice mail, cell phones, e-mail and the internet are effective sales tools when utilized properly. However, when you prospect none of these mechanisms should be operational. If you use an account management tool, such as ACT or Siebel (both are highly recommended), make sure you use these databases offline. This will eliminate any temptation to respond to e-mail or to surf the internet.

Stand up when you make phone calls

Physically, your voice sounds more imposing when you stand. When you talk leaning back in a relaxed position, your voice is more sluggish. Also, standing during a phone call keeps you more alert.

Smile into a mirror

People can tell when you smile on a phone call. It's like standing. You are more effective and more pleasant. A mirror will remind you to smile.

Don't hunt for elephants

It's important you don't spend your time on opportunities that will not make you or your company money. However, nothing is more dangerous than only looking for the "big one." Large deals (those that are at least three times your monthly quota) take much longer to close and are much more work. Salespeople who spend all their time searching for elephants tend to perform erratically. Their monthly numbers are up and down and they jump from company to company. Consistent reps are much more valuable. Would you rather have one huge deal every six months and no sales in between, or five consecutive months of mid-sized deals that are worth more overall?

"It is better to sell a large number of cars at a reasonably small margin than to sell fewer at a large margin of profit ... It enables a large number of people to buy and enjoy (the car) and gives a large number of men employment at good wages. Those are two aims I have in life."

Henry Ford

Have fun!

Some reps like prospecting more than others, but few love it. Prospecting is a means to an end. When you realize how much closer prospecting brings you to that big commission check, you will like it more. But there are things you can do in the interim to make it more tolerable. Start by having fun.

Make a game of it. Pair up with a partner at the office. Bet colleagues how many buildings you can get thrown out of ... or how many people will hang up on you.

Prospecting is like making new friends, meeting strangers for the first time or the first date. The anticipation can be exciting and scary. But the results can be spectacular.

Don't take rejection personally

When people treat you rudely, 99% of the time the reasons have nothing to do with you. The odds are they are having a bad day, something bad just happened or they are angry at the world. People who take out aggressions on innocent sales reps are so insecure and bitter that they have nothing better to do than to be mean to strangers. Laugh at them. Pity them. Don't get upset. Why waste the energy?

People refusing to hear your ideas and people rejecting you are two very different things. Recognize the difference.

One day, early in my career, I cold called an office. Wearing a suit and tie and carrying a briefcase, it was clear that I was a salesperson. But before I could even say, "Hello, my name is …" the woman at the front desk interrupted. She ordered me to leave and threatened to call security. Perplexed, but recognizing my presence was not the reason for the outburst, I decided to turn my negative experience into an opportunity to break the ice with my next encounter at another business.

"Hello, my name is Todd and I'm with USN Communications," I told my next opportunity. "Please don't yell at me. I just left a potential customer downstairs who almost took my briefcase and threw it at me before I could even get two words in."

"Really?" my nice new friend said. "That didn't happen to be XXX Company, did it?"

"Yes," I replied with a smile. "As a matter of fact, it was. Do you know the woman?"

"No," she responded. "But I do know they were robbed at gunpoint two days ago by a stranger claiming to be a sales-person."

Establish numeric maximum and minimum goals

Have goals for your prospecting time. Your maximum goal should be nothing short of making the sale on every call. On a more realistic level, set numeric goals. For instance, you may want to make 50 phone calls, reach 10 decision-makers, have 10 hang-ups by secretaries, leave 20 voice mails, have 5 conversations with decision-makers and schedule 5 appointments. Don't limit the goals to how many phone calls you make and how many appointments you schedule. We will explain this further in a moment.

The more specific you are, the more effective you are.

Track your numbers

We discovered earlier that the reason Tiger Woods is so successful is that he knows exactly what he needs to do to be successful. You can do the same. Know your numbers every day. Not only should you know how many appointments you schedule, but you should understand your own skill set to the point that you can anticipate what will happen on every sales call and prospecting call. You can do this if you know your "ratios." Earlier we established an "Expect Excellence!" list for you. To obtain your overall financial goals, we decided you needed to adhere to specific weekly activity goals. To ensure you are on track, you need to analyze this progression further.

By tracking your numbers, you can determine how many phone calls you need to make to reach how many live decision-makers. You can determine how many "hang-ups" by decision-makers you need to have to ensure you get a firm appointment.

Professional prospectors recognize every "no" is one step closer to a "yes."

If, for three weeks straight, 10 people hang up on you or kick you out of their office during a cold call, but you conclude each week with a sale, then the hang-ups become part of your success. If days go by when you don't get hung up on and it looks like you will not achieve your formula for success, then you should become concerned. Go find some people to hang up on you!

The following page is a "Daily Tracker." Copy and use it every time you prospect. It will serve as a manager when you have no manager. When properly used, this is a remarkable tool.

First, adjust the categories as you see fit. As you finish calls, enter numeric slashes under the appropriate category. At the end of the day, the Tracker will allow you to easily summarize your prospecting successes and to track the events that lead to each success.

DAILY TRACKER

Date of prospecting (Cold Calling/Telemarketing/Networking/Referrals)

_____

Appointments scheduled

Nice conversations with secretaries and left voice mail

Left voice mail – direct line

Blow-offs by gatekeepers (gave a business card, got a card, hung up by secretary)

Blow off from decision-maker (hung up, no interest)

Hot interest from decision-maker – follow-up plan (no firm appointment – send info)

Sit-down appointment with decision-maker, follow-up plan (next appointment scheduled – 10 minute talk)

Sit-down appointment with decision-maker but never, never land ("call me whenever")

Networking voice mail

Networking scheduled appointment

Networking sit down appointment

Networking blow off

Count with numeric slashes how many times each event happens (e.g., ⁄⁄⁄⁄⁄)

Know who you are calling ahead of time

If you are door knocking (making unannounced in-person visits for the first time), know precisely where you are headed. Know the exact address of the building and how to get there. Don't spend time driving around. You will prospect nobody.

If you are calling via telephone, print your entire list before picking up the phone. Don't make a call, then take a break to look up a number, make a call, take a break, etc. Momentum is everything.

Have everything you need to close the sale with you

Remember that your optimal goal is always to close a sale.

"It is better to be prepared for an opportunity and not have one than to have an opportunity and not be prepared."

Whitney Young, Jr.

If you are door knocking, be as prepared as you would be if you were conducting a scheduled appointment. Have contracts, pricing, date book, etc. with you on the initial call (see the following page for a checklist). If you are telemarketing, have everything you would have if you were in a direct meeting with the person on the phone with you.

Be organized. Don't ever be in a position where you have to call back potential customers because you don't have information that you left at the office.

Everything I Need to Have when I Prospect

- Pen
- Pad of paper for notes
- Datebook (electronic or written)
- Business cards
- Pricing (all pricing)
- Contracts (necessary documents requiring signatures)
- Internal paperwork (demonstrating to customers what's required on your end)
- Product samples (either physical or pictures)
- Presentations (electronic or written)
- Testimonial letters about your company
- Testimonial letters about you
- Media articles about your company
- Media articles about your company's industry
- Color brochures about your company
- Color brochures about your product
- Written guarantees your company or product offers
- "What (Your Company) Can Do for You" (will explain later)
- Company Contacts (will explain later)
- Personal Profile (will explain later)

Decide how to prospect

How will you prospect? Will you telemarket? Will you make in-person cold calls? Will you scan newspapers? Will you network?

The following is a list of various resources and techniques for earning new clients. These will vary depending on your industry. Later we will discuss in detail how to utilize many of these prospecting resources.

Where to find prospects

- Customers
- Friends/Relatives (Is there anyone who wants to help you more?)
- Door knocking (unannounced in-person visits)
- Telemarketing (unannounced phone calls)
- Territory by city, state or zip code
- Target a particular industry
- Target a company size (by revenue or number of employees, etc.)
- Library databases, such as Sorkin's
- Competitor customer lists
- Vendors (anybody you do business with, including your accountant, attorney, insurance agent, web designer, local phone provider, long distance phone provider, cell phone provider, office equipment provider, health club, landlord/condo association, barber, grocery store manager, dry cleaner)
- Media articles about companies or "Movers/Shakers" ("I'm calling in response to the article about you in ... I wanted to congratulate you. We work with companies like yours ...")
- Members of Associations in which you or company have memberships
- Members of Chambers of Commerce in which you or company have memberships
- Members of Chambers of Commerce in area in which you live (even without membership)
- Alumni of high school or college

Introduce and humanize

The three most powerful strategies in sales are smiling, saying a person's name and using the word "help."

"Hello, So-and-So, can you help me?" humanizes a situation by connecting you with whom you are speaking. We all love acknowledgement. "Is Todd there?" "Todd, how are you today?" "What's up, Todd?" I get goose bumps just writing the words!

Now, add the word "help." "Can you help me, Todd?" "Todd, can I trouble you for some help?" "Todd, I really appreciate your help."

People want to help – even the most cynical of people. But people really only want to help when they perceive themselves as helping. Everyone wants to give the homeless man on the street money – **if** they think he deserves it. Everyone wants to donate money to charity – **if** they believe in the cause. Giving to others is human nature. Consider parenting. To be a parent, you must believe in giving yourself.

When prospecting, introduce yourself, ask them to introduce themselves and ask for help on the initial contact. Say your name and the name of your company. Then repeat the other person's name aloud. Remember, this is a first call. You never know with whom you are speaking. Perhaps this is the owner's daughter, the owner's son, the owner's spouse. Perhaps you are talking to the owner, who is filling in at the front desk during a lunch hour.

Imagine this scenario:

Salesperson: "Can I speak to the person in charge?"

Counter person: "I am the person in charge! What? You think because I sit at the front counter, I have no responsibility?"

Add humor wherever possible. In prospecting, personality is very important. This is where you "earn the right to sell."

Icebreakers for prospecting

"Hi there, how are you doing? Oh, all right. I know that look. You're thinking, 'Quick, head for the hills. Here comes the salesperson. Act busy."

"All right, I surrender. I admit it. I'm a sales-person. Shoot me dead in my tracks now and get it over with."

"Hello, how are you? Look, do me a favor and just talk to me. This is the 10th call I've made in the last hour. I've been hung up on 10 times and had my brochure ripped up 10 times. It's been a long day!"

(If they have a sliding glass window up front) "Can I have a cheeseburger and fries?"

"Oh, So-and-So is not here now? He probably knew I was coming and ran away."

(If they do not laugh at all at any of these jokes) "Oh, come on. That was a little funny, don't you think?"

Explain why you selected this particular company

Everyone wants to be "chosen." No one wants to be called upon just because you are cold calling. Even if you actually are cold calling, there's a reason you found this organization. Maybe it is its location, the type of industry or the company size. Tell prospects *why* you chose them.

- If someone referred you, immediately say "So-and-So referred me."

- If the company is a similar business to other clients of your company, then say, "We've been doing work with company Such-and-Such. We thought we'd see if we could help you, similar to the way we are helping them."

- If the company is part of your geographic territory, then say, "We've been doing work with company Such-and-Such in this area. We thought we'd see if we could help you, the way we are helping them."

Companies are like individuals. They want to be acknowledged for their unique characteristics. No one wants to be picked at random.

State Initial Benefit

Remember that killer initial benefit statement from last chapter? It's now time to use it – on every person you meet. Here's an example of how it can help you.

Once, when I was a sales manager, a sales rep and I knocked on doors. We approached a company and the secretary greeted us. Rather than barreling her over asking for the decision-maker, we stated our initial benefit. Before she could respond, a man approached. He indicated he had overheard our pitch. "Phone service? Did you say phone service? Your timing is very good," he said. "But I missed the beginning of what you said. What exactly do you do?" We stated our initial benefit statement again. Another man approached. He, too, overheard the conversation. "Phone service? Did you say phone service? Our internet is down as we speak," he commented.

Two weeks later we signed the deal. And two years after that, Technomic International became the first TBN Sales Solutions client.

Ask for appointment

While rapport building and humanization are critical parts of prospecting, scheduling and running appointments are necessary to close deals. If you don't ask, you won't receive. After stating your initial benefit statement, explain that you would like to talk further during a formalized meeting.

Here is a suggested script:

> "I'd like to schedule an appointment with you and whoever else also makes the decisions in this matter to see if we can help."

Let the person you are speaking with guide you to the person in charge. At this point you do not know who is the decision-maker. Although you may have an idea (the CEO, CFO or Controller), companies differ. If the person you are speaking to is confused and says, "It's not me. I'm not sure who that would be," then suggest a title, such as CFO, CEO or Controller. However, let the prospect recommend first. The person you are speaking to knows more about their company than you do. Let *them* recommend the person in charge.

Empower

In most cases, when it comes to prospecting, you won't meet the people you need on your first unannounced visit or phone call. Like you, most people are very busy and hard to reach. They are even harder to reach because you do not know their schedules, nor do they have a relationship with you. However, the person with whom you are speaking is the opposite: This person knows schedules and has relationships with the people you seek. Take advantage. They often know whether their company will be interested in your service. Build an alliance with them. Empower them. Often decision-makers decide whether to speak with you based on a secretary's opinion.

The people you speak to know more about their company than you do. Let them recommend the person in charge.

For instance, say this:

> "Perhaps you could help me. I realize So-and-So is the one who actually makes those decisions but your job is very important, too. Are you familiar with your company's services in this area? Who do you use? What do you have? Do you think So-and-So would be interested in our programs? What do you think would excite So-and-So … so that he would become interested in our services? If the decision were up to you, would you consider us? I'd really appreciate the *help.*"

Secretaries and receptionists are integral parts of the sales process.

Never take "no" from someone who can't say "yes," but recognize that those who can only say "no" often possess the knowledge to share with you what it would take to get a "yes."

Close for appointment

When you finally reach the person with whom you want to speak, close for an appointment then and there. While you are a top notch consultant, the fact is, by the very nature of your visit, you are intruding. It was not scheduled. If prospects are ready to meet on the spot, great! However, be aware that being ready to meet and giving you five minutes to hear what you have to say are two different things.

Prospecting is not about prospects hearing what you have to say. It's about discovering their needs to determine whether you can help.

Here are some basic rules when it comes to scheduling appointments:

- Never conduct an appointment standing up

It's a negative sign if prospects are not willing to physically sit down with you in a meeting, even if they say they are interested. "This is fine," they might say. "Let's chat right here."

Don't do it.

Your job is to generate enough interest to create an opportunity. Opportunities only happen when both parties are willing to sit down to engage in a conversation. A good measure is to never stand up chatting more than five minutes.

If the prospect appears interested, then ask permission to continue at that moment. Say, "I know I came by unannounced, but it sounds like we may be in a position to help your company. Do you have at least a half hour to chat right now? If not, let's schedule an appointment."

If they say 'yes,' they will automatically invite you into their office or a conference room. Congratulations! You just shortened the sales cycle.

If they indicate they don't have the time, the next step is to schedule a future appointment – at that precise moment.

Here's a recommended script:

> "I'm glad you're interested, So-and-So. But this
> information is very important and I don't
> want to review it by the seat of our pants. I'd
> be wasting your time and my own. They are
> equally valuable. Let's schedule something.
> How's Thursday at 9 a.m.?"

- Schedule the appointment right then and there

Don't say that you'll call next week to schedule an appointment. Do it right there, even if it's a tentative appointment. Pull out your date book. Suggest a date and time based on your schedule. You asked to meet so you should decide when. If the prospect can't meet on your terms, compromise.

- Qualify

Some salespeople erroneously believe that once you schedule the appointment, you should leave right away. They fear prospects will change their minds.

Prospects who change their minds about meeting with you do so because they were never interested in the first place.

Make sure the prospect meets *your* criteria. Does the prospect meet your target revenue? Does the prospect meet your target employee number? What kind of timeframe is the prospect working on? If a prospect has no intention of switching phone providers for two years, don't schedule a meeting now. An *introductory* meeting might be beneficial, because if the prospect's situation changes you want to be the first person the prospect thinks of to contact. But be smart.

Another reason why it's important to qualify is that sometimes prospects will meet with you knowing they have no intentions of utilizing your services. They only do so because they want to obtain pricing information from your company to use as leverage against their current vendor. Their goal is for their current vendor to lower its prices – at your expense.

A good example of these kinds of prospects are ones who have stiff penalties if they switch providers. It's important to ask these prospects point blank, "If you would incur a $1 million penalty by switching away from your current vendor, and you only spend $3,000 per month, what's the purpose of meeting? I know I wouldn't switch if I were you ... unless there's more to the issue."

Buyers are not liars – when you ask the right questions.

- What is the role of the individual?

In the ideal world, salespeople always meet with people who can sign on the dotted line. They spend their time with the decision-makers exclusively. But sometimes, it's just not possible. Meeting with someone who only recommends is fine as long as you know that prior to your meeting. The fact that they are not the decision-maker is valuable, because now you can tailor your conversation accordingly. For example, you wouldn't ask someone to sign an agreement if you know that person does not have the authority. However, you would try to build an alliance with this individual so that when it comes time to sign the agreements, you have this person selling your service to the decision-maker.

- Confirm – but not the way you think

There are two schools of thought about confirming meetings. One says to never confirm, because you give the prospect a chance to cancel. The other says to always confirm, because your time is valuable. Do confirm appointments, but do it in a way that won't make it easy for the prospect to cancel. This way you are valuing your own time, while reducing the chance of cancellations. Say this:

> "I'll tell you what, So-and-So. Here's what I'll do next week. The day before our appointment, by noon at the latest, I will send an e-mail confirming our appointment. I don't want to waste your time or mine. They are equally valuable. And I don't want to be one of those annoying sales reps always calling to confirm. I will leave the ball in your court.

> "After I send the e-mail, if anything comes up or you change your mind for whatever reason, all I ask is you contact me to cancel. Is that fair?

> "But, if I don't hear from you after I send the e-mail, I will assume no news is good news. You will see my smiling face at xxxx on xxxx. How does that sound?"

Do's and don'ts of prospecting

In-person

• Dress business casual

Business casual is less threatening when you call in-person, because most of the time your first contact will not be with the decision-maker. The people you talk to probably won't be wearing suits and ties. If you dress like them, subconsciously they will feel less threatened. Now you seem more like a "regular person" rather than the dreaded "salesperson." Also, most salespeople still wear business attire, so dressing casually sets you apart from the crowd. If available, wear a casual shirt with the company logo. Then, not only are you casual, you are a walking advertisement. People appreciate others in uniform.

• Always get a business card

Don't settle for an envelope or a piece of stationery. If that's all the receptionist offers, then accept it. However, don't settle unless you absolutely have no other choice. Business cards have e-mail addresses, faxes, web sites and formal titles. Without them, you may have to interrogate the secretary to acquire the necessary information. You might say:

> "I appreciate the envelope, but if you have a card, that would be great. It *helps* keep me organized."

• Always leave a business card and one-page brochure

Prospects may be interested, if there is something for them to be interested in. A business card says who you are and where you work. A brochure is a written verification of why the prospect should care.

• Take notes on the company's business card, including who you spoke to, the date and potential buying criteria

It's priceless to be able to return to the office and call the following day saying, "Is this So-and-So? We spoke yesterday. I'm following up on our conversation. Is John there? "

On the phone

• Leave a voice mail saying your name, your company, phone number, your initial benefit statement, and then your name and number again

Nothing is more annoying than listening to a long message and not understanding who is calling or how to contact that person. Leave your name, company name and phone number, immediately followed by your initial benefit statement. Conclude again with your name and phone number.

Here's an example:

> "This is Todd Natenberg, president, TBN Sales Solutions, 773-755-1306. I'm calling to see if we can help. TBN Sales Solutions increases commissions for salespeople and profits for businesses through customized training, coaching and consulting. We establish structures and procedures in all facets of the sales process, through classroom workshops and individual sales coaching, to teach reps to control their own destinies, thereby impacting the bottom line. I want to see if we could *help*. Please call me. Again, Todd Natenberg, TBN Sales Solutions, (773) 755-1306. Thanks very much."

Recently, I called a prospect who I had not spoken to in more than a year. It turned out my contact had since left, but I left a voice mail saying who I was, why I was calling and stated my initial benefit. Two weeks later, a woman from that company called to say the company was interested.

"Hello, Todd,'" the woman said. "My name is Diane and I am returning a call you left on our machine trying to reach Susan. Susan is no longer here, but we are now exploring sales training programs for our company, as you indicated you offer. Please call me."

Summarizing, the steps in prospecting are:

1. Prepare.

2. Decide how to prospect.

3. Introduce and humanize.

4. Explain why you selected this particular company.

5. State Initial Benefit.

6. Ask for appointment.

7. Empower.

8. Close for appointment.

Treat every person like they can sign on the dotted line.
For all you know, they can.

CHAPTER 5

Obtain Referrals

Referrals: An effective way to earn business in which one individual endorses the services of another individual to a third party in an effort to increase everyone's income

Don't question why someone would refer you. Question why they would not.

What *are* referrals? How and when do salespeople obtain them? Why is there no better way to earn clients?

Referrals can take many forms. In the ideal world, new prospects contact you to indicate they have a strong interest in your service because So-and-So referred you. They are contacting you because they have an explicit need that must be filled immediately. Someone they respect very much told them you could fill that need.

Does this happen? Absolutely. Does it happen frequently? Absolutely not. A more common referral is when salespeople ask permission to utilize either an existing customer's or prospect's name to earn the business of another opportunity. In these cases, the person whose name is being used sometimes will call the new opportunity ahead of time to inform this person you will be calling.

But how do you get people to refer you business without paying them? How do you get them to voluntarily share their name to help make you more money?

Top salespeople always ask everyone for referrals. They always give everyone referrals.

The steps to obtaining referrals are:

1. Prepare.

2. Who do you ask?

3. What do you ask?

4. Qualify.

5. Utilize the referral.

6. Create your own referrals

Prepare

Sound familiar? Do you notice a recurring theme? In all aspects of sales, preparation is essential. To execute each strategy successfully, you need to create the proper mindset and assemble the physical tools ahead of time.

To effectively obtain referrals, you must believe you offer valuable services. People who refer business to you are not just doing you a favor. Recognize that when you get referrals, the person who does the referring benefits as much as you. If all goes according to plan, they, too, will receive accolades. For instance, when customers refer you to their clients to poten- tially provide local phone service for them, and the service benefits everyone, your customers shine as brightly as you! Your customers have made it clear they are looking out for their clients' best interests in more ways than one.

Sometimes salespeople don't ask for referrals for fear they will "bother" their customers. If you think your service is a bother, find a new service to sell.

There will be situations periodically throughout your sales career when you ask for referrals and your customers refuse to help you. They may say, "I would never do *that* to someone I know." When that happens, laugh. Note the absurdity of the comment. A fair response would be this:

"**Never do what?** You would never share with someone an incredible product you have purchased that will help their business? You would never help someone you care about improve their business?"

If you were in the market for a new car, and your friend knew a terrific salesperson but did not refer you, how would you feel? Your friend knew this salesperson would be fair, friendly, very competitive about price and would take care of all your needs. However, your friend never mentioned this salesperson, because he didn't want to "do *that* to you." So you venture into the scary world of buying a car on your own. You encounter the stereotypical salespeople: fast-talking, plaid-suit-wearing individuals only out to make a buck at whatever cost to the consumer. You leave the shopping experience emotionally deflated.

Would you thank your friend for not "doing *that* to you?" Of course not. You'd be upset that your friend did not share valuable information.

Who do you ask?

Contrary to some some salespeople's views, referrals do not only come from existing customers after the service or product is delivered without any errors. If referrals could only be garnered that way, none of us would achieve success. To best obtain referrals, identify available resources. Even if someone or a company is not a candidate for your service, they may be able to refer you to someone who is.

Obtaining referrals involves telling many people what you offer in many ways. The objective is that when someone talks about the type of product you offer, yours is the name that comes to mind.

Who can refer me?

- Customers
- Prospects
- Friends/Relatives
- Internal employees
- Vendors
- Office equipment vendor
- Office supplies vendor
- Your accountant
- Your attorney
- Your insurance agent
- Your local, long distance, cellular phone, web hosting, internet provider
- Your health club
- Your landlord/condo association
- Your barber
- Your grocery store manager
- Your dry cleaner
- Members of Associations in which you or company have memberships
- Members of Chambers of Commerce in which you or company have memberships
- Members of Chambers of Commerce in area in which you live (even without membership)
- High School and College Alumni organizations
- Previous employers
- Past internal employees from previous employers
- Previous prospective employers
- Competitors
- Salespeople who sell to the same clients in the same territory, but with a different product
- Salespeople who sell a complementary product in the same industry (e.g., phone equipment vendors referring phone service providers)
- Leads groups (More on these later)

Let's highlight some of these referral opportunities. We will delve into more detail about the rest in the upcoming Networking chapter.

• Customers

Reconsider the philosophy that the only time to ask for referrals is when a product or service is delivered flawlessly. What if, by chance, your company's delivery is not perfect? Does that mean you are not entitled to a referral? Of course not! Mistakes happen. If salespeople limit themselves to times of errorless perfection, they miss out on tremendous opportunities.

Upon the actual signing of the agreement

The best time to ask for referrals is not after delivery, but when the agreement is signed. Do you think your customers have any doubts about what they just agreed to purchase? If they did, they wouldn't have bought. Often, it's more exciting to anticipate receiving something new than to actually receive it.

Here's a suggested script for the "signing of the agreement" scenario:

> "Thanks very much, So-and-So. I'm excited to start servicing your account. In the interim, perhaps you could help me further. You know how hard jobs are like ours. Who do you know who may be able to benefit from our service as much as you will very soon? It would really *help* me."

Upon delivery of the service

When a product is delivered flawlessly, do ask for referrals. Just note this is not the only time to ask.

> "So-and-So, it looks like we delivered on our promise. Perhaps now you could help me further. You know how hard jobs are like ours. Who do you know who may be able to benefit from our service much as you have? It would really help me."

Upon resolution of a crisis

---

*"The pessimist finds the difficulty in the opportunity.
The optimist finds the opportunity in the difficulty."*
Winston Churchill

Sometimes the best times to get referrals are those times when the most goes wrong. Some salespeople mistakenly believe that customers expect there to not be a single problem ever with their product or service. Customers are not foolish. They know errors occur. Mistakes happen. What they desire – demand – is that the issue be addressed professionally and resolved as quickly as possible with minimal damage to their business.

In times of crises, customers judge you on how quickly you return phone calls, whether you keep them informed and how you utilize resources beyond your ordinary duties. If you manage to do all of the above, take advantage of the situation. Say this:

> "So-and-So, I know things did not go exactly as planned. However, hopefully, you saw our ability to resolve problems. Just as I helped

you, perhaps you can now help me. You know
how hard jobs are like ours. Who do you
know who may be able to benefit from our
service like you have? It would really help
me."

- Vendors

Anybody you pay for services or products should – without
hesitation – be willing to at least consider giving you business.
If their company is not a candidate for your services outright
(maybe they're too small or not your target market), they
should consider referring you to those who do qualify for your
programs. But you must ask. Vendors are not in the mindset of
perceiving you as the seller and them as the buyer. They see you
as the client. Reverse this perception. Say this:

"So-and-So, I need your help. You know how
hard jobs are like ours. Since I have been
your client during this time, I was wondering
if you might be interested in our services and
enable me to return the business. Or, who do
you know who may be able to benefit from
our service? It would really help me."

- Prospects

Salespeople will sometimes "click" on a personal level with
prospects, but still do not earn the business. These prospects
will tell you "how good you are," "how much they like you" and
how their decision to not purchase your services is "nothing
personal."
Ask them for referrals. Say this:

"So-and-So, I know we are not in a position to
help you and your company at this time. But
perhaps you could help me another way. I'd
greatly appreciate it. You know how hard jobs

are like ours. Who do you know of who may
be able to benefit from our service? It would
really help me."

- Internal employees

This includes all non-salespeople such as administrators,
customer service and sales support. These people have many
connections, and already believe strongly in your company and
your product. (They work with you!) Helping you bring in business makes them look good. It does not matter that they don't
get commissions. Often, generating revenues for the company
and for someone on their team is incentive enough. Take them
to lunch. Buy them gifts. Appreciate them.
Say this:

"So-and-So, I was wondering if you could help
me. You know firsthand how good our
company is and the service we offer. You
know how great our customer service is
because that's you. Who do you know who
may be able to benefit from our service? It
would really help me."

- Friends/Relatives

Take advantage of friends and family. They want to see you
succeed.
Say this:

"So-and-So, I was wondering if you could help
me. I know we are in different business
worlds, but you know how hard jobs are like
mine. Who do you know who may be able to
benefit from our service? It would really help
me."

What do you ask?

Getting good referrals takes work. It goes beyond, "Do you know someone?" There are steps to be conducted:

- Personalize

Referrals are not about your company. They are about you. No one refers a company. They refer individuals. Even if your referrer likes your company, you want them to focus on referring you personally.

- Ask for *help*

- Specify what kind of company you target

People can't help you if they don't know how.

When you ask for referrals, define your ideal client. Give examples. The easier you make it for people to refer you, the more they will. For instance, when TBN Sales Solutions asks for referrals, we return to the top characteristics of our ideal client. On sales calls we explain that "ideal" candidates (although we don't limit ourselves to these) are companies with the following characteristics.

- They employ between 5 and 20 salespeople.
- Typically, they have never had sales training.
- They receive some commissions or bonuses.
- They are a new business.
- Their current process is geared around growing accounts, rather than earning new clients.
- Their decisions are made by CEO or VP of Sales.
- They are based in Chicago.
- They are startups/less than 5-year-old companies.

- – Their revenues are between $5 million and $50 million.
- – Examples include mortgage brokers, AXA Advisors, Relcon Apartment Finders, CyberSearch, Ltd. (all are well-known names in Chicago).

Make it easy for people to give you referrals. The easier it is, the more you will get.

To continue with what to ask:

- Ask open-ended questions such as "Who can you refer me to?"

By asking an open-ended question, you force the person to come up with an answer. Often that answer will be "Such-and-such comes to mind …"

- Ask the referrer to go the extra mile

Get greedy. Don't accept only a name and a company name. Ask the referrer to make a phone call to alert the person you will call. Do not let the referrer tell you that the other person will call you. It's critical that you be able to contact that person. If we all waited around for people to call us, none of us would have jobs. Ask for a name, the company name and an e-mail address.

Qualify

Sometimes qualifying can be a challenge. You don't want to bombard the person referring you with questions but, "If you shoot for the stars and settle for the moon, that's okay, too." Ask your new best friend questions to qualify the referral.

You might ask, "Why do you think they'd be interested? How big is the company? Have they ever had sales training?" Your referrer may not know the answers, but if they do, you have an added bonus. The more information you have when you contact prospects, the stronger your position.

Here's how it may sound:

Salesperson:	"So-and-So, I was wondering if you could help me. You know how hard jobs can be like mine. Perhaps you could refer me. Who do you know who might be looking for sales training or sales coaching?
	"The ideal candidate for me is a company much like yours, with a sales force between 5 and 20, typically a new company or a startup, one that has salespeople who are not traditional outside salespeople with 10 years experience.
	"One of my clients is CyberSearch. They are a recruiting company where I did a series of workshops for their 10 reps. Another is Relcon Apartment Finders, a free apartment finder service. Who do you know with similar traits?"
Referrer:	"Why don't you call Company XYZ? Mention my name."
Salesperson:	"That's terrific. I really appreciate it. But now I am going to get greedy. Could you leave them a voice mail telling them I will call? This is what I will say when I call: 'This is Todd Natenberg. So-and-So referred me. I don't want to get So-and-So in trouble for providing your name, but he thought perhaps I could help your company, because we target organizations like yours.'
	"How does that sound? Thanks very much."

Referrer:	"No problem."
Salesperson:	"One more thing, what do you know about their business? What's So-and-So like...?"

Utilize the referral

Some salespeople receive referrals, but fail to maximize the referrals' potential. They receive names and numbers of companies to call, but then when they contact the potential customer, they fail to mention how they received the referral's name. Why?

"I didn't want to make the person who referred me mad at me for mentioning his name," the salesperson explains.

Here we go again. Mad at you? Referrers voluntarily provided you company name and information. They did so because they wanted to help you. They felt you deserved it, and were willing to wield their own influence to see you succeed. They also thought you legitimately could help someone they respect. They wanted to share that with their colleagues.

What does it say if someone else feels you and your service can help others, but you don't think you and your service can help others?

Another reason salespeople do not maximize utilization of referrals is that they do not recognize the value of saying someone referred them. There are two reasons saying someone else's name is powerful:

1. Your new contacts may not know or like you, but they do know and like your referrer. Often, that's incentive enough to hear you out.

2. These contacts will be flattered someone else was thinking of them and their needs.

Early in my career I sold phone service to individual distributors of a network marketing company that operated in a similar fashion to Amway. The company produced a special vitamin drink to boost energy. The first customers I signed up were Joe and Carol. They came to me because my sister-in-law worked with them.

Over the next six months, I signed up 10 more of these network marketers in Joe and Carol's chain. Each time the business came from Joe and Carol's referrals. Each time, I used their name. Each time, the sale took five minutes. The response was always the same. "If Joe and Carol referred you, you must be good. Sign me up."

When utilizing referrals, there are some important rules to follow:

- Lead with the name of the person who referred you

Don't just "mention" their name. Say it first. The person who referred you is your in. The name could singlehandedly ensure the contact will listen to your initial benefit statement. Also, indicate how you know them. If they're a client, say so. If they're a prospect, say the prospect is considering your services or that you are "working with them." If you network together, say that. Relationships are important.

- Phone first

As important as e-mail may be, the phone is more personal. The sound of one's voice and hearing another's name stimulates the mind more than e-mail, especially at the beginning of a business relationship.

- Continue to follow the "Steps in Prospecting" in Chapter 4

Although you will lead with the person's name who referred you, in the eyes of the person you contact it's still a cold call. Some salespeople wrongly assume just because this is a referral, they can ignore steps like asking secretaries their names or stating their initial benefits.

One difference is that now you will ask directly for someone – before stating your initial benefit – rather than let the secretary indicate who's in charge. Here's a sample script:

Salesperson:	"Hello. My name is Todd Natenberg and I'm the president of TBN Sales Solutions. What's your name?
	"Nice to meet you, So-and-So. The reason I'm calling is AAA referred me to John at your company. Is John in?"
Secretary:	"No, he's not. Can I take a message? What's this regarding?"
Salesperson:	"The reason I'm calling is TBN Sales Solutions …"

Often, the conversation the salesperson has with secretaries and receptionists when utilizing referrals is just as critical as the conversation they will have with the person they actually want to meet. If the salesperson upsets the message-receiver, your contact could care less who you know.

• Voice mail is your friend

We spoke earlier about always leaving voice mail messages when prospecting. With a referral, request voice mail if the person you are contacting is unavailable. You can leave a message with the secretary, too, but for the referral to have its utmost power, it's important the person you are contacting know you are not cold calling. Often, the secretary will not relay this vital information. You want that person to actually hear your voice and the name of the friend who referred you. You want them to know who told you to call, why they told you to

call and why they should care that their friend told you to call.
Here's a sample script for the voice mail message:

> "Hello, So-and-So. This is Todd Natenberg,
> President, TBN Sales Solutions, (773) 755-
> 1306. So-and-So from Such-and-Such
> referred me. They thought I could help your
> company. My organization increases
> commissions for salespeople...."

• E-mail if you can't reach them

Don't think just because contacts don't call you back, they
aren't interested. People are busy. You need to create a sense of
urgency. Creating a sense of urgency comes in part from
making your message clear, concise and available by all means
possible. E-mail is one of these means.

But be careful. With referrals, following up can be a little
tricky, because there is more than your reputation on the line
now. How you conduct yourself is a direct reflection on the
person who referred you. Persistence is still key, but tread care-
fully. The best way to avoid seeming overly aggressive is using
e-mail.

Here are some rules to adhere to:

• If the referral does not call back within three days, send e-
  mail referencing your unsuccessful phone attempts

• The e-mail must begin with the name of the person who
  referred you

• Say exactly why you are sending information

• Enclose information

• Blind cc those who referred you

People love to help when they know they are helping. Nothing is worse for referrers than when they give leads to salespeople and never hear back about the lead. The salesperson should always say thank you and give the referrer the courtesy of keeping them informed about the status of the opportunity.

A client once told me he had referred a mortgage broker named Bob to one of his friends, Susie, but never heard anything back. He figured nothing came of it. Six months later, a mutual friend informed him that Susie indeed signed with Bob for a mortgage deal two months prior.

My client was livid. How could Bob not let him know? A simple thank you would have been nice, since my client had just referred Bob $2,000 in commissions! "How hard would it be to e-mail me a thank you?" my client asked. "Even easier, Bob could have blind cc'd me on e-mail correspondence between him and Susie!" The client made it clear he would never refer Bob again. He actually wished he hadn't in the first place.

If people refer you, practice common courtesy by keeping them informed about the status of the opportunity. By keeping them up-to-date, they also can continue to help you land the new client.

How powerful would that be if the next time Susie and my client spoke, my client asked Susie about the status of Bob's deal.

"Oh, you know about that?" Susie might ask.

"Of course," my client replies. "I referred you to Bob. How's he doing?"

"Fine. I guess. I'm just not sure … I'm glad you brought it up. I actually have a couple questions for you …"

In contrast, what would my client's reaction be if Susie asked first about the Bob deal?

"Oh, you're still working with Bob?" my client would reply. "I had no idea. I figured because I never heard from him, nothing came of it."

The more people who know what you are doing, the more people you have to help you do what you are doing.

Here's a sample letter for your files.

Sample Referral E-mail

Subject: So-and-So referred me – Skyrocketing sales for XXX

Prospect So-and-So (always use their first name),

So-and-So recommended I contact you.

My name is Todd Natenberg and I am the president of TBN Sales Solutions, as well as the author of the book *"I just got a job in sales. Now what?" A Playbook for Skyrocketing Your Commissions.*

I know So-and-So, because …

Since I have been unable to reach you via phone, I'm sending e-mail to introduce TBN Sales Solutions as a way to skyrocket sales for XXX.

TBN Sales Solutions increases commissions for salespeople and profits for businesses through customized training, coaching and consulting. We establish structures and procedures in all facets of the sales process, through classroom workshops and individual sales coaching to teach reps to control their own destinies, to impact the bottom line.

I also have enclosed materials for your convenience. I encourage you to visit www.toddnatenberg.com for more information.

After you have had a chance to review the materials, I would like to schedule an in-person appointment to review your needs. I will call you on Tuesday.

Please call (773) 755-1306 or e-mail todd@toddnatenberg.com with questions.

Thanks for the consideration. I look forward to speaking with you on Tuesday.

Sincerely,
Todd Natenberg
President

TBN Sales Solutions
711 W. Gordon Terrace, Ste. 106
Chicago, IL 60613
Phone: 773-755-1306, Fax: 773-442-0840, Outside Chicago: 866-464-0339
e-mail: todd@toddnatenberg.com
http://www.toddnatenberg.com

TBN Sales Solutions increases commissions for salespeople and profits for businesses through customized training, coaching and consulting. We establish structures and procedures in all facets of the sales process, through classroom workshops and individual sales coaching, to teach reps to control their own destinies, to impact the bottom line.

• Call again

Your job is not done yet. You said in the letter you would call on a certain date. Call. If you get voice mail once again, leave another message complete with your initial benefit. Remind the contact that you promised you would call on this date per your e-mail and that is why you are calling. If you still don't get a response back, move on and put the prospect in your tickler file.

Create your own referrals

When salespeople speak of referrals, they typically mean someone else providing you a lead for a business to contact. In the ideal world, that person to whom you are being referred is the decision-maker, the company is qualified and the person is expecting your call. But if sales were that easy, everyone would be in sales.

Think how successful you would be if you treated every opportunity like a referral. What would that do to your confidence? How would those you call on feel if you made it clear you chose them from the thousands of companies in the marketplace? A referral is really just an explanation of why you are calling on someone. Some are better reasons than others. But any reason can qualify as a referral.

Salespeople may tell prospects they do business in a common geographical area, in the same industry or with companies of the same size. Isn't that a referral? Rarely would the salesperson say this:

> "Hello, my name is Todd Natenberg and I'm the president of TBN Sales Solutions. I know nothing about your company, what you do or why you'd be a good candidate for our services. I picked up the phone book, closed my

eyes and boom, your name came up. Would
you like to consider our programs?"

Actually, if salespeople did say this, the decision-maker
might meet with them out of sheer respect for their upfrontness
– or they may meet just because they found the salesperson
amusing. But since we know this is not what ordinarily
happens, let's take advantage of what we will call "self-made
referrals."

If you discover an opportunity because of an article you
read in the newspaper, the newspaper is your referring agent. If
you are contacting members of the Chamber of Commerce
because you are a member, the Chamber is the referral source.
Who says referrals come only from human beings?

Scripts for self-made referrals

• Territory by zip code, city or region

> "Hello, Prospect So-and-So. My name is Todd
> Natenberg. I'm the President of TBN Sales
> Solutions. The reason I am calling you is we
> do work with companies like yours in this
> city, such as So-and-So. I thought I'd contact
> you to see if we can help you the same way
> we are helping So-and-So.
>
> "TBN Sales Solutions increases commissions
> …"

• Vertical market (by industry, revenue size, employee size,
etc.)

> "Hello, Prospect So-and-So. My name is Todd
> Natenberg. I'm the President of TBN Sales
> Solutions. The reason I am calling you is we

do work with companies like yours in your industry/of your size/, such as So-and-So. I thought I'd contact you to see if we can help you the way we are helping them.

"TBN Sales Solutions increases commissions …"

- Customers of a struggling competitor

    "Hello, Prospect So-and-So. My name is Todd Natenberg. I'm the President of TBN Sales Solutions. The reason I am calling on you now is to update our records. Our information indicates you have company XXXX for services. Is that correct?

    "Yes? Well, the reason I'm contacting you now is to educate you on changes in the industry. While I hate to bash competition, we do pride ourselves on keeping consumers informed. You should be aware of the situation at company XXXX.

    "If this is a concern, I would like to volunteer our services as an alternative.

    "TBN Sales Solutions increases commissions...."

Be careful with the latter scenario. No one likes competition-bashing, but prospects do appreciate your educating them about industry changes. If a company is having financial difficulties, for example, it tends to lose customers for this very reason. Just be sure you act professionally.

- Memberships – Chambers of Commerce/ Professional Associations/Churches/Synagogues/College Alma Maters

  > "Hello, Prospect So-and-So. My name is Todd Natenberg. I'm the President of TBN Sales Solutions. The reason I am calling you is that, like you, I'm a member of XXXX. I'm contacting you to see if we can help your company – from one member to another.

  > "TBN Sales Solutions increases commissions …"

- Customer/prospect organizations memberships

  > "Hello, Prospect So-and-So. My name is Todd Natenberg. I'm the President of TBN Sales Solutions. The reason I am calling you is we do business with other companies in your association, such as company XXX. I'm contacting you to see if we can help your company, like we helped company XXX.

  > "TBN Sales Solutions increases commissions …"

- Industry articles in the media about your prospect or your prospect's company (Promotions/Movers and Shaker/In the News)

  > "Hello, Prospect So-and-So. My name is Todd Natenberg. I'm the President of TBN Sales Solutions. The reason I am calling you is I saw the article in XXX publication. Congratulations on the exposure.

"We do business with companies like yours. I'm contacting you to see if we can help.

"TBN Sales Solutions increases commissions …"

Referencing the media works well to get to the person in charge because the secretary often thinks you are calling as a potential client, not as a potential vendor. What's also great about this method is that there is nothing shady about it. You never indicated you were interested in buying this company's services, only that you are contacting them because of the article. You are doing just that.

Referencing also is a compliment. Even the shyest people like attention even if they don't admit it.

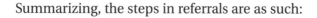
Summarizing, the steps in referrals are as such:

1. Prepare.

2. Who do you ask?

3. What do you ask?

4. Qualify.

5. Utilize the referral.

6. Create your own referrals.

Referrals are much more than a name and a number. They are qualified opportunities that are mutually beneficial to not only the salesperson, but the person doing the referring as well.

CHAPTER 6

Build the Business Case

Sales Call: An appointment with a firm date and firm time with the goal of uncovering prospects' needs, desires and hot buttons to provide solutions that result in the advancement of the sale

Customers do not care how much you know until they know how much you care.

You have organized yourself. You have earned the right to sell through building rapport and empowering the gatekeeper. You have created interest by stating your initial benefit in an articulate and effective manner. You have solidified the appointment with a firm date and firm time. All of these steps have been the build up to this moment: Running the sales call.

Through your previous strategies, you have positioned yourself as not just another salesperson. You've made it clear you are a consultant. To continue the process effectively, you must now show how much you care. This means learning about prospects. It means asking questions to uncover needs. Your goal now is to "build a business case." If all goes as planned, the business case will demonstrate why the prospect would be crazy not to purchase your product.

In this chapter, we will present the playbook for building a business case, otherwise known as running a sales call:

1. Prepare.

2. Send PAL (Purpose/Agenda/Limit).

3. Introduce to gatekeeper.

4. Research while waiting.

5. Set the agenda.

6. Reposition.

7. Probe.

8. Summarize.

9. Present.

10. Close.

Prepare

Preparing for a sales call is a little more straightforward than preparing for prospecting, but there are similarities.

Write down minimum and maximum goals

Unless you know ahead of time that you are meeting with someone who can't approve your purchase, your maximum goal, again, is to close the sale. Your minimum is to obtain commitment to a follow-up appointment with a firm date and firm time.

Have everything you need to close the deal with you

Even if you are sure there is no chance of closing, treat the appointment like it is a closing. The things you should have with you were explained in Chapter 4, but the list is worth repeating because of its importance.

Everything I Need to Have on a Sales Call

- Pen
- Pad of paper for notes
- Datebook (electronic or written)
- Business cards
- Pricing (all pricing)
- Contracts (necessary documents requiring signatures)
- Internal paperwork (demonstrating to customers what's required on your end)
- Product samples (either physical or pictures)
- Presentations (electronic or written)
- Testimonial letters about your company
- Testimonial letters about you
- Media articles about your company
- Media articles about your company's industry
- Color brochures about your company
- Color brochures about your product
- Written guarantees your company or product offers
- What (Your Company) Can Do for You" (will explain later)
- Company Contacts (will explain later)
- Personal Profile (will explain later)

A few items on this list are important enough to note again:

- Contracts (filled out ahead of time)

Ask experienced salespeople if they've ever been on a call without contracts with a prospect who was ready to sign. Watch them cringe as they answer. Nothing is worse than a customer saying "Yes," but you have to say "No." Even if you think there is no chance of the deal closing, be prepared. No matter how complex the sale, have contracts with you.

While some information will need to be filled out with the prospect present, fill out what you can ahead of time. Details such as the name of your customer, phone number, etc., should be completed prior to the meeting. It's not pushy. It's professional. Prospects actually expect you to ask for the order. They certainly expect you to be prepared for the order. They know you are in sales. Surprise!

Filling out paperwork prior to the meeting also saves valuable time. Don't frustrate prospects to the point where they won't buy because they don't have the time to fill out the paperwork.

- Extra business cards (for referrals)

Not only are you there to earn this client, you are a professional who will request referrals. Have extra business cards with you at all times.

- Datebook

If the prospect wants to meet again, be ready to schedule. If you want to meet the prospect again, be ready. Professionalism is everything. Don't guess. It looks better to fill in your datebook than to write it on a piece of paper. Having your calendar in front of you also prevents you from double-booking meetings.

- Written records of account

This includes e-mail correspondence, past proposals, company information, such as that found on the prospect's web site, and any miscellaneous handouts the prospect has given you. It's important that you and the prospect are on the same page. Don't expect the prospect to have your information nicely organized. It's your job to have your information nicely organized for the prospect.

Send PAL prior to the meeting

Of all the tools and selling strategies in this book, none is more effective than the PAL: Purpose, Agenda, Limit. The PAL is not the ordinary agenda that many salespeople claim they send ahead of time. The PAL is a confirmation, an outline, an affirmation of logistics, and a preview of what you and your prospects intend to discuss at a meeting. It's a very powerful tool.

When I worked for LCI International in suburban Chicago, I once scheduled a meeting with the owner of a lumber company. I sent the PAL prior to the meeting. When I arrived, the prospect said, "I don't remember who you are, but I got your fax [no e-mail back then]. Obviously we spoke and I just forgot. But I was so impressed with this form that I now have to consider switching to LCI. And I want you to know I am having each of my sales reps send these to their prospects."

Sample PAL

First Appointment

Subject: Skyrocketing sales for XXX – Agenda for Friday meeting with TBN Sales Solutions

So-and-So,

This memo is to confirm our appointment tomorrow, Friday, December 27, at 2 p.m. at your office in Arlington Heights, 3295 XYZ Rd., (555) 555-5555. If anything has changed, please call me on my cell phone at (773) 791-2360.

Per our conversation and previously with YYY, who referred me to you, I am confident after your evaluation you will agree we offer the best programs available in today's sales training industry.

Purpose:

To review potential ways to help skyrocket revenues through the retention of services provided by TBN Sales Solutions.

Agenda:

• Learn more about XXX

• Examine sales training goals and needs

• Review TBN Sales Solutions programs relating to these goals and needs

• Sign necessary paperwork to hire TBN Sales Solutions

Limit: 1 hour

Attending:

So-and-So, (555) 555-5555

Todd Natenberg, President, TBN Sales Solutions (773) 791-2360

Sincerely,

Todd Natenberg
President

TBN Sales Solutions
711 W. Gordon Terrace, Ste. 106 Chicago, IL 60613
Phone: 773-755-1306, Fax: 773-442-0840, Outside Chicago: 866-464-0339
e-mail: todd@toddnatenberg.com http://www.toddnatenberg.com

TBN Sales Solutions increases commissions for salespeople and profits for businesses through customized training, coaching and consulting. We establish structures and procedures in all facets of the sales process, through classroom workshops and individual sales coaching, to teach reps to control their own destinies, to impact the bottom line.

Let's examine each section.

- **Subject: Skyrocketing sales for...**

Treat the subject line like it is your initial benefit statement. From the beginning, plant the idea that your goal is not just to meet with your prospect. Your goal is to help their business. Other good catch phrases, depending on your preferences, include "Impacting the bottom line," "Increasing efficiency" or "Increasing revenues." Don't be boring. Act with excitement and your prospect will, too. But don't fall into the trap of being so excited that you forget to tell the prospect why you are meeting.

One of the great benefits of e-mail is its organizational record-keeping ability. However, not enough people take advantage of this. Too many managers write "read this" in the subject box. How on earth is a salesperson, or a prospect, supposed to locate specific information by the "read this" category? Isn't all e-mail sent with the plan that recipients will read the message? If we don't expect it to be read, why send it? "Read this" is also dangerous because often spammers use this for subject lines.

The easier salespeople make it for their prospects to be organized and attentive to their services, the more attentive they will be.

- **This memo is to confirm our appointment on Friday, December 27, at 2 p.m. at your office in Arlington Heights, 3295 XYZ Rd., (555) 555-5555. If anything has changed, please call me on my cell phone at (773) 791-2360.**

As we indicated earlier, never confirm appointments via phone. Avoid putting yourself in a situation where you are engaged in voice mail tag to determine whether you are meeting with prospects. Leave the ball in their court. Give them the power to cancel the meeting with the understanding that if they don't cancel, the meeting is on.   Also, these sentences provide important logistics. They tell where you are meeting, the time of the meeting and how to reach one another. When driving to the meeting you now have all the information readily available. If for any reason the location has changed or you misunderstood information, it can easily be clarified. Everyone is held accountable.

- **Per our conversation and previously with YYY, who referred me to you, I am confident after your evaluation you will agree we offer the best programs available in today's sales training industry.**

Remind your prospects how you came to them, especially if it's a referral. They will appreciate having their memories refreshed. Even with a PAL in hand, more than one prospect will ask you at the start of a sales call, "Who are you again? How did you find me? What are we discussing?"
In addition, now the prospect can thank YYY for referring you in the first place. We agreed last chapter that referrals benefit everyone.

- **Purpose: To review potential ways to help skyrocket revenues through the retention of services provided by TBN Sales Solutions**

Unless expressly spelled out, your agenda may not be the prospect's agenda. The "purpose" establishes you as a professional who has a specific plan, ensures that your purpose is the same as the prospect's and eliminates surprises for both of you.

- **Agenda:**
  - Learn more about XXX
  - Examine sales training goals and needs
  - Review TBN Sales Solution's programs relating to these goals and needs
  - Sign necessary paperwork to hire TBN Sales Solutions

Now you are a true professional. You know what you want to achieve and how you want to achieve it. You've made it clear that this meeting is about the prospect, not you. You have stated your desire to learn more about the prospect's wants and needs. At the same time, you've made it clear you are there as a salesperson to earn a client.

One of the reasons that salespeople often have a tough time closing deals is they worry that they will come across as too pushy. But when prospects meet with salespeople, they expect the salesperson to try to earn their business. In fact, during my sales management days, more than one prospect told me the only reason they did not buy my sales rep's services is the salesperson did not ask for the business.

If prospects are truly not ready to sign, they will e-mail or call to alert you that "signing paperwork" will not happen at this juncture.

When that happens, respond, "No problem. I appreciate you being upfront, but let's still meet. Frankly, that's why I sent the agenda. I wanted to be sure we are on the same page. Now I know where we stand. See you Friday."

No one likes to be sold, but everyone likes to buy.

- **Limit: 1 hour**

Tell the prospect how much time to budget. One hour is recommended. Some sales managers and trainers will ask for

15 or 20 minutes, but be careful about estimating low. When was the last time you ran a true sales call in a short 20 minutes? Be realistic. If you put a time limit, stick to it. Don't ask for 20 minutes if you know you need an hour.

- **Attending:**
  So-and-So, (555) 555-5555
  Todd Natenberg, President, (773) 755-1306

Have you ever been on a sales call where you brought along your sales manager, the sales engineer and the customer service person, and someone had to stand because there was not enough space? That situation would be easily avoided had you let the prospect know beforehand who would attend.

Also, if you alert prospects that you are bringing your manager or specialist, they can decide if they want to invite others from their company. If you are not sure if someone will be there, add "???" after the name. Bringing managers impresses prospects because it shows you value their business.

Always underpromise and overdeliver – never the other way around.

The following pages include other sample PALS.

Second Appointment - Present Proposal

Subject: Skyrocketing sales for XXX – Agenda for Friday meeting with Todd and TBN Sales Solutions

So-and-So,

Hope all's well.

This memo is to confirm our appointment tomorrow, Friday, December 27, at 2 p.m. at your office in Arlington Heights, 3295 XYZ Rd., (555) 555-5555. If anything has changed, please call me on my cell phone at (773) 791-2360.

Purpose:

To finalize a program to help skyrocket revenues through the retention of services provided by TBN Sales Solutions.

Agenda:

• Update on XXX's sales training goals and needs

• Review TBN Sales Solutions programs relating to these goals and needs

• Questions? Issues?

• Sign necessary paperwork to hire TBN Sales Solutions

Limit: 1 hour

Attending:

So-and-So, (555) 555-5555

Todd Natenberg, President, TBN Sales Solutions, (773) 755-1306

Sincerely,
Todd Natenberg
President

TBN Sales Solutions
711 W. Gordon Terrace, Ste. 106 Chicago, IL 60613
Phone: 773-755-1306, Fax: 773-442-0840, Outside Chicago: 866-464-0339
e-mail: todd@toddnatenberg.com http://www.toddnatenberg.com

TBN Sales Solutions increases commissions for salespeople and profits for businesses through customized training, coaching and consulting. We establish structures and procedures in all facets of the sales process, through classroom workshops and individual sales coaching, to teach reps to control their own destinies, to impact the bottom line.

Phone Appointment

Subject: Skyrocketing sales for XXX – Agenda for Friday meeting with Todd and TBN Sales Solutions

So-and-So,

This memo is to confirm our phone appointment tomorrow, Friday, December 27, at 2 p.m. I will call you at (555) 555-5555 at that time. If anything has changed, please call me on my cell phone at (773) 791-2360.

Per our conversation and previously with YYY, who referred me to you, I am confident after your evaluation you will agree we offer the best programs available in today's sales training industry.

Purpose:

To further review the potential solution to help XXX skyrocket their revenues through the retention of sales services provided by TBN Sales Solutions

Agenda:

• Update of sales training goals and needs of XXX

• Further review of TBN Sales Solutions' programs relating to these needs

• Verbal commitment to hire TBN Sales Solutions

• Schedule dates of TBN training

• Schedule appointment to sign paperwork to hire TBN Sales Solutions

Limit: 1 hour

Attending:

So-and-So, (555) 555-5555

Todd Natenberg, President, TBN Sales Solutions, (773) 755-1306

Sincerely,
Todd Natenberg
President

TBN Sales Solutions
711 W. Gordon Terrace, Ste. 106 Chicago, IL 60613
Phone: 773-755-1306, Fax: 773-442-0840, Outside Chicago: 866-464-0339
e-mail: todd@toddnatenberg.com http://www.toddnatenberg.com

TBN Sales Solutions increases commissions for salespeople and profits for businesses through customized training, coaching and consulting. We establish structures and procedures in all facets of the sales process, through classroom workshops and individual sales coaching, to teach reps to control their own destinies, to impact the bottom line.

Networking Appointment

Subject: Skyrocketing sales for XXX – Agenda for Friday meeting with Todd and TBN Sales Solutions

So-and-So,

This memo is to confirm our appointment tomorrow, Friday, December 27, at 2 p.m. at your office in Arlington Heights, 3295 XYZ Rd., (555) 555-5555. If anything has changed, please call me on my cell phone at (773) 791-2360.

Per our conversation and previously with YYY, who referred me to you, I am confident after your evaluation you will agree we offer the best programs available in today's sales training industry.

Purpose:

To review mutual networking opportunity to help So-and-So and TBN Sales Solutions skyrocket revenues for both our companies

Agenda:

• Who is So-and-So? What does the company of So-and-So do?

• Who is Todd Natenberg? What does TBN Sales Solutions do?

• Consider mutual networking opportunities

Limit: 1 hour

Attending:

So-and-So, (555) 555-5555

Todd Natenberg, President, TBN Sales Solutions, (773) 755-1306

Sincerely,
Todd Natenberg
President

TBN Sales Solutions
711 W. Gordon Terrace, Ste. 106 Chicago, IL 60613
Phone: 773-755-1306, Fax: 773-442-0840, Outside Chicago: 866-464-0339
e-mail: todd@toddnatenberg.com http://www.toddnatenberg.com

TBN Sales Solutions increases commissions for salespeople and profits for businesses through customized training, coaching and consulting. We establish structures and procedures in all facets of the sales process, through classroom workshops and individual sales coaching, to teach reps to control their own destinies, to impact the bottom line.

While the PAL is important for all appointments, for the networking meeting it is essential. When you send an agenda prior to a networking meeting, you are a true professional. The person with whom you are meeting can't wait to swap leads. They think if you take networking that seriously, you must take selling just as seriously.

Using the PAL does not mean appointments will never cancel. They will, but unusually they will cancel prior to the meeting. The prospect will send e-mail or call to inform you of a change in plans. That's okay. Better to get the cancellation prior to the meeting than to go out and meet with someone who's not really interested.

On the rare occasion that you do go to meet with a prospect and the prospect is nowhere to be found, a printout of your PAL becomes your greatest tool. Here's how it works when the meeting has been canceled without your knowledge.

Salesperson:	*(showing your PAL to the secretary)* "I'm so sorry. I even confirmed the appointment. Here's a printout of the e-mail I sent. I hope everything's okay. I certainly was not trying to intrude, but when I did not hear from So-and-So, I thought we were on. See?"
Secretary:	"No, I'm the one who's sorry. That's unlike him. Let me get him on his cell phone. That's not right."

In most cases, prospects feels so guilty about your professionalism and their lack of professionalism, they want to reschedule a solid appointment. "It's my fault," they say, more often than not graciously apologizing. "I know I should have called. Can we reschedule it? What works for you?"

Introduce yourself to the gatekeeper

You are prepared. You've sent your PAL to confirm the meeting. The only thing left is to conduct the appointment. You arrive at your prospect's place of business – and a receptionist out front tells you to wait in the lobby. This is not actually a prospecting visit, but treat it as such. Approach the receptionist as you would on a blind cold call, although you don't need to state your initial benefit.

If you've been here before and you know the receptionist, be just as friendly as you were the last time. Greet the receptionist by name, shake hands, provide a business card and tell her with whom you have an appointment. Be sure to say you have an appointment at the appointment time. Some front desk people question salespeople unnecessarily. If the person you are scheduled to meet is on the phone, they may refuse to interrupt. This can pose a problem because time can pass while the prospect remains on the phone. It's a never-ending circle. Usually prospects only stay on the phone because they don't realize you are waiting outside. The longer you wait, the more upset they grow, thinking you are late.

If this happens, politely, but sternly, say, "If you could just please tell So-and-So I'm here, I'd appreciate it. We are slated to meet at XXX. I've had it happen more than once that customers remain on the phone or in a meeting because they think I'm not here. I appreciate the help."

It's bold, but necessary. Stand your ground.

Research while waiting

While waiting, observe your surroundings. Take stock of the magazines on the table. Stand up and read the awards on the wall. If you see photographs, take note. Look for commonalities between what you see and your own life or profession. Do you like the architecture of the office? Is there a view of the lake? Are there articles about the company on the table? What about a company newsletter? Build your arsenal. This will be important in a moment.

Reintroduce

At last, you and your prospect are meeting face to face. How you act in the next 20 seconds will determine how long this meeting lasts and whether your prospect will be interested. Take nothing for granted:

- Say hello with a firm handshake and a smile

- Give the prospect a business card

If there is a walk back to the office, take stock of your surroundings like you did in the waiting room. What's on the walls? Are there awards? Are there customer service letters? Observe the prospect's office as you sit down.

If this is a referral, reference how the two of you have a mutual acquaintance. If it's not a referral but you know the same people, acknowledge the commonality.

Humanize

Like prospecting, don't jump right into a discussion of what you are selling. Build rapport. Some suggestions include:

- Comment on what you saw outside the office

- Refer to the conversation with the receptionist

- If something exciting happened on the way in, tell the story

- Discuss current events

- Reference any mutual acquaintances you might have

When humanizing, read the prospect. While you are not a psychologist, reading people is a large part of a sales job. Your goal is to be as much like the prospect as possible. Be yourself, but cater to prospects' needs. Physical and emotional commonalities have been proven to be very effective.

Practice "mirroring," otherwise known as mimicking. If the prospect talks fast, you talk fast. If they want to get down to business, you get down to business. If they cross their legs, you cross your legs. Subconsciously, it will put them at ease. But don't overdo it.

People like to do business with people who are like them. Be as much alike as you can.

Questions to ask yourself before the meeting begins to assess the person with whom you are meeting

- Does the prospect initiate the handshake or was it a response to your action?
- Is it a firm handshake?
- Does the prospect offer a business card first?
- Does the prospect have a pad to take notes?
- Where does the prospect have you sit?
- Are you in an office or a conference room?
- Are you across from the prospect's desk?
- Does the prospect talk fast or slowly?
- Does the prospect make eye contact?
- Does the prospect show emotion?
- Does the prospect talk technically?
- Does the prospect share personal information or is it all business?
- Is the prospect impatient?
- Does the prospect look at the clock regularly?

Interpret what you've observed. For example, a firm hand-shake means a confident professional. If they give you a business card right away, that often indicates they are all about business. They don't want to chit chat. You need to tell them what they want to hear. If prospects sit next to you, they often want to get to know you, not just your company. If they have a pad to take notes, they are probably serious about considering your services.

Set the agenda

Pull out two print-outs of the PAL. Give the prospect a copy and keep one for yourself. Again, having two copies is professional. Summarize what you wrote. Don't assume your prospect will remember. Include how long you expect the meeting to last.

Here are some specific words to use. The purpose will vary depending on the kind of meeting. Refer to your PAL for this. But the beginning should be consistent:

> "Thanks, So-and-So, for meeting with me. I'm glad our schedules could match up. I don't want to waste your time or mine. They are both equally valuable.

> "What I would like to do is learn more about your company, including what you are looking for in the areas of sales training if anything. Then I'd like to tell you a little bit about TBN Sales Solutions as it relates to your needs. If there's a potential fit, we'll go from there.

> "This meeting should take no more than an hour. If it goes longer, though, because you are asking good questions and there's an

> interest, then you can't kick me out. How
> does that sound?"

This immediately puts you on the same professional level as the prospect. Tell them upfront that their time is no more valuable than yours. Say it politely, but with confidence. Prospects will appreciate you taking your own job seriously. Also, note the length of the meeting. Just because you sent an e-mail saying the meeting will take one hour, don't expect prospects to remember. Things may have come up. Perhaps prospects do not have an hour now. Perhaps they have more. The best way to find out is to ask.

Don't be afraid to cancel a meeting if you suspect it will not go according to plan, even after you are seated in front of your prospect .

If a prospect appears worried or distracted, ask the prospect what's wrong. Perhaps something occurred prior to your arrival that has diverted the prospect's attention from your meeting. If this is the case, offer to reschedule. It's a tough thing to do, but your prospect will appreciate it in the long run. Better to waste your drive time than to sacrifice two hours of opportunity time.

You can say...

> "Is everything okay, So-and-So? It seems like
> your heart is not in this and that your mind is
> on other things. I can appreciate that. I'll tell
> you what ... this information we are
> reviewing is very important. I don't want us
> to rush through the materials. That won't
> help either one of us. Why don't we
> reschedule this for another time?"

Knowing when to walk away is sometimes just as important as knowing when to proceed.

Reposition

Before asking questions directly, remind the prospect why you are here and what you are discussing. Reposition yourself and your company. Don't assume that, just because you spoke for an hour on the phone last week, the prospect will remember the conversation. Repositioning entails the following:

- Say you are here to ask questions

- Say how you came to be here – referrals, etc.

- Remind them of the past discussions, including dates and circumstances

- Restate initial benefit

> "I have a bunch of questions for you, but before we get into that, let me just remind you in a nutshell what we do and how we came to meet. As I indicated, So-and-So referred me to you. He's a customer of mine. He thought we could help you the way we are helping him. To refresh your memory, TBN Sales Solutions … (initial benefit statement)."

- Pause

Let prospects digest what you say. See if they have any questions. But be cautious. All you are looking for is a nod of the head. You actually don't want the prospect to bombard you with questions at this point. You want to do the bombarding. You want to gather information from the prospect, not have the prospect gather information from you.

Another reason to pause is to evaluate the prospect. Watch the prospect's reaction. It will help as you forge ahead. If the prospect jumps in with "I just want to know the price," it's very telling. Don't immediately respond, but do alter your style to focus more on business.

Probe

Frequently clients ask how I happened to go from being a reporter to a salesperson to a sales manager to a sales trainer. Actually, journalists and salespeople have very similar personalities. Like journalists, salespeople must be thick-skinned. They encourage people to talk and share their wants and desires. Salespeople, too, must be curious and appreciate the power of information. A reporter develops an "angle" for a story based on interviews; a salesperson develops a "solution" based on questioning. In the world of sales, this questioning is called "probing."

Probing is like a flow chart. Asking certain questions achieves another result, then another result, and so forth.

The key to effective probing is to build from easy, non-threatening questions to challenging questions in which you create "pain."

Let's return to our example of prosecuting attorneys. What if they immediately attacked defendants with accusations? "You did it! Didn't you? Admit it! Admit it! Admit it!" Generally, attorneys first coddle the defendants. They earn trust ... then they work on the defendants to obtain a confession.

In probing you want to accomplish the following:

- Build alliances to tie back during the presentation

- Reveal the buying criteria prospects will use

- Understand the prospect's buying process

- Make prospects feel pain so they desire a solution before one is presented

- Uncover two or three main hot buttons (things that excite and motivate them) that will enable you to present a solution accordingly

Let's take these one at a time:

Build alliances to tie back during the presentation

Think about your best friend. Why is that person your best friend? The two of you undoubtedly have things in common. You may not have identical interests, but perhaps your values are the same, your religion is the same or you may have grown up in the same neighborhood. Similarities are a large part of why you connect. Selling is no different.

One of my first clients was a small computer company. At the time I sold the account, I was going through a divorce. Ironically, so was the prospect, although I did not know it at the time. One afternoon, we had a sales meeting to analyze his phone bill. It was getting late and my prospect still hadn't decided whether to purchase. He told me to call him next week, because he had to meet with his attorney to discuss his pending divorce.

"I know what you mean," I replied. "I'm going through a divorce right now. What a nightmare."

"You 're having a nightmare?" he replied. "You want a nightmare? Let me tell you what this thing is costing me ..."

Ten minutes later, we had a signed deal.

Don't worry. Divorce is not the only way to build alliances with your prospects. More conventional ways include having similar target clients, such as both of you targeting small and mid-sized businesses, earning customers through referrals, or sharing similar keys to success, such as providing top-notch customer service.

Ascertain information to build alliances which you ultimately will tie back later in the presentation.

Reveal the buying criteria prospects will use

If you do not know what prospects will base their buying decisions on, how can you sell to them? What you think is important and what prospects think is important don't always coincide. Studies have proven that, contrary to popular belief, people do not buy on price in most cases. But if you ask salespeople why they lose deals, many will tell you it was because their price was too high. Often, the real reason wasn't that the price was too high, but rather that prospects didn't find the solution cost-effective.

If everything was based on price, there would be no need for salespeople. If you sell on price, you lose on price.

There are situations where the lowest per unit cost makes or breaks the opportunity, but let prospects say this aloud. Don't say it for them. Think about your own buying habits. Do you always buy the least expensive product? When we say "least expensive," what are we comparing it to? If something is the cheapest but it does not meet our needs, who cares what it costs?

Two years ago I bought a new car. I was looking for a black, four-door Honda. The salesperson showed me a black, four-door Honda. However, the price tag included shampooing the car mats and repolishing the car. These added items would cost me $500, but I did not need them.

"I'll throw it in," the salesperson offered.

"But I don't want them," I contended.

"I'll throw it in," he repeated.

"I guess if you are willing to lower the price by $500, then okay," I answered.

"No," he answered. "But I said I'd throw it in."

When I told him I was confused, he said he'd "throw them in" for cost. This meant the car's value increased by $500, according to him. "But I don't want the shampooing," I answered angrily.

"I'm throwing it in," he foolishly argued.

I tried an analogy he would understand. "Do you play golf?" I asked. "Let's say someone offers to sell me a set of golf clubs for $10. That's an amazing price for an entire set of clubs. But it's not a good deal if I have no arms or legs!"

Understand the prospect's buying process

As we indicated earlier, never ask prospects if they are "the decision-maker." Often, they may think they make the decisions, when the fact is someone else has to approve the purchase. A better question is:

"Who signs on the dotted line? Is that you?"

Again, it doesn't mean you shouldn't meet with this person, but how you approach the meeting will differ. You won't try to close an opportunity and get a signature when it's been established from the onset this person can't sign any binding agreements. Likewise, if prospects say they do sign, but at the end of the meeting they need to run it by someone else, call their bluff.

"When I asked you earlier, you said you signed. Did I miss something?" ask them.

- Make prospects feel pain so they desire a solution before one is presented

Former President Bill Clinton once said, "I feel your pain." This comment enabled Clinton to touch the emotions of the American public. It played a critical role in his election to the presidency.

When pain is felt, we want it to go away. If we can't make it go away, we look for help to make it go away.

In the training world, some refer to this technique as "cut and gush." It refers to discovering a problem, then making the prospect feel the problem more and more – to the point where prospects can't stand it anymore. The result is they **must** find a solution. Amazingly, you seem to have one.

Selling is like digging into the depths of the human soul, uncovering individual feelings and emotions, then trying to satisfy these feelings and emotions.

At TBN Sales Solutions, we often help companies who have salespeople who aren't running as many appointments or closing as many deals as is necessary to achieve the organization's revenue goals. When we press prospects, the conversation may go as such:

Prospect:	"It's not really that big a deal."
TBN:	"No big deal? What does that do to your bottom line if you are paying people who are underperforming?"
Prospect:	"We lose money, I suppose, but it's really not that much."
TBN:	"How much is not that much? Do you have a dollar figure? $10,000? $20,000?"

Prospect: "Oh, it's much more than that. Yes, I guess, it is a bigger problem than we care to admit."

In probing, uncovering a problem is not enough. Prospects need to not only agree with you, but to verbalize these feelings. In other words, they need to create the problem.

When people verbalize their feelings, they believe it. When you verbalize their feelings, they question it.

The following pages have questions to ask on a sales call. Make copies to use when conducting your interviews.

Building Your Business Case

Prospect: _____

Contact Information: _____

Date of Meeting: _____

General Information "Nice Questions"

1. Before we get started, I was wondering if you could help me. Every customer is different with different needs. I don't want to waste my time or yours. They are both valuable. What I really want to find out is what's important to you. To do that, I am going to ask you some questions. Is that fair?

2. In your own words, tell me a little about your business.

3. Who is your target customer?

4. How do you get clients?

5. What do you think has been the key to your business success?

6. What separates your business from others in your industry? (They will almost never say the lowest price!)

7. What are the goals of the company? Growth?

8. What is your position and responsibilities?

9. How did you come by this position? What's your background?

Building Your Business Case (cont.)

Buying Process "Not as Nice Questions"

1. Please walk me through the buying process. Who signs on the dotted line if we do earn your business? Is that you?

2. Forget my company for a minute. If you were to make a decision, what kind of timeframe are you looking at? When would you want our product – anyone's product – installed and up and running?

Current Vendor "Challenging Questions"

1. What do you think of your present vendor?

2. What's your biggest challenge with the present vendor?

3. How would you rate your vendor on a scale of 1-10 with 10 being the highest? Why are they not a 10?

4. Oh, you had a problem? What happened?

5. What did that do to your present business?

6. How much do you think that cost you in money? Time? Aggravation?

TBN Sales Solutions, 773-755-1306, www.toddnatenberg.com

Building Your Business Case (cont.)

7. What would that do to your business if you treated clients that way?

8. What do you define as good customer service?

9. What criteria did you use the last time you made a large purchase? How did it go?

Specific Product Information (Varies by product and industry, but you will need this information)

The Best Question to Ask!

Prospect So-and-So, I only have one other question for you. Like I said earlier, each of my clients are different with different needs. I have a lot of information I could go over with you about our company and what we offer. But for you to use our services and our programs, all I want to know is what else is important to you?"

How many questions you ask depends on the rhythm of the sales call. The questions are not the important part – the answers are. Many of these questions may be answered without being asked. If the prospect volunteers information, jot down the answers and check off the questions. Return to why you probe: to build alliance, uncover hot buttons, etc. Let your prospects verbalize the information.

But what if you have prospects who want to cut to the chase because of time? The prospects are interested, but view your questions as socializing. If this happens, ask one and only one question. If you cannot get the answer to this one question, end the call and move on. You are wasting your time.

> "Fair enough, Prospect So-and-So. I only have one question for you. Each of my clients are different with different needs. I have a lot of information I could go over with you about our company and what we offer. But I don't want to waste your time or my time. They are equally valuable. For us to earn your business in this area, what is important to you?"

Don't beat around the bush or change the words on this one. Don't say "What are you looking for?" The words, "important to you"are extremely powerful. They evoke an instant sense of caring, respect and sincerity. The answer also will tell you what you need to know.

Summarize

This is an easy way to distinguish yourself, because few salespeople do it. Be sure you understand the answers to all your questions. Prove that you listened, not just heard. What's the difference between listening and hearing? Hearing is simply not being deaf. But listening entails a three step process.

At TBN Sales Solutions, we call it the ART method:

- Acknowledge

- Repeat

- Take action

Acknowledge

Have you ever had a one-way conversation where you do all the talking? Isn't that just as annoying as when someone else does all the talking? You feel like you are talking to a brick wall. Then, when you address the situation, what's the other person's response? "I heard you. What was I supposed to say? I didn't know it called for a comment." What the other person doesn't understand is that you wanted acknowledgement. You needed to understand they heard your words.

Ways to acknowledge include nodding your head with direct eye contact, positive or negative facial expressions depending on the situation and verbal comments, such as "I understand" or "I know what you mean." Acknowledge.

Repeat

Typically, when salespeople acknowledge a prospect, they feel they've listened. But this is just the first step. The second step is actually repeating what was just said to ensure you interpreted it properly. Returning to our newspaper reporter analogy, how is it that two reporters can attend the same press conference, hear a source say the same thing and write about it differently in each newspaper? This happens in spite of the fact both reporters have tape recorders! It's because one hears and the other listens.

The best way to avoid this problem is to repeat exactly what you hear. Don't dissect every sentence. Just hit the high points. If you did not get every point down, repeat what you remember.

In hearing you repeat it, the prospect will be so impressed that what you leave out won't matter.

Take Action

This proves you truly understand the prospect's needs. What you say or do next must be a direct response to the answers provided. Many sales reps have lost deals or won deals at this step. Here's an example of what not to do.

During my corporate training days, a rep and I probed one prospect with good questions. We reached the point where the prospect told us, "What really matters to me is reliability and customer service. Price is not the issue. If you can guarantee me your company can provide these two criteria, you will earn my business."

The rep's response was, "Great, let me show you how we can save you money. By switching to us, we will lower your rate."

The meeting ended 10 minutes later. We never heard from the prospect again.

Listen.

Here's some suggested wording:

> "Okay, Prospect So-and-So. Let me summa-
> rize what you said. You have been with the
> company for 10 years. You came here from
> Idaho because you found it to be a great
> opportunity. One of the key reasons for the
> company's success is customer service. Your
> company sells to small and mid-sized busi-
> nesses. You are the one who would 'sign on
> the dotted line.' What is important to you
> now is billing, customer service and a
> competitive price. Is there anything I left out

in terms of what's **important to you** and your company?

"No? Then let me tell you how we can help."

Present

It's finally your turn to talk. So what do you say? How will your product and company help this prospect based on all the information you just ascertained? You properly pointed out there's a problem. It's your job to prove you know how to fix it.

You don't want to sound as if you're reading a script, but a written presentation is necessary at this point. An effective presentation will answer the following:

- Who is your company?

- Why and how it has been successful?

- Who are you?

- Why and how have you been successful?

- What is the product you are offering this prospect to fix the problem?

- How will this product fix the problem?

- What does it cost?

- Sign here!

When presenting, have as many visuals as possible to answer the above questions. Remember our philosophy about seeing things: When we see it, it becomes real. This is similar to setting goals. You are not the only one who believes something more when it is written down. Your prospect will, too.

Some suggestions for a top-notch presentation follow.

What to include in your presentation

- PowerPoint™ arranged in plastic sheets in a leather binder
- A laptop presentation – if financially feasible
- Product samples (or, if you're selling large equipment such as photo-copiers, bring pictures)
- Brochures about every product you offer
- Written guarantees
- Testimonials about you and your company
- Your profile
- Pricing
- Contracts

Your presentation should be one section of your "site-seller" which is what holds the "Everything You Need to Close a Deal." Other valuable presentation tools to include are:

- Internal paperwork (Prospects appreciate seeing what you do after you sign them up. It also helps if you need to gather additional information at a later date.)

- Industry articles about your services

- Contacts at your company

- One-page implementation procedure detailing delivery of your products

- One page sheet of "What (Your Company) Can Do for You"

Here are samples of brochures we use at TBN Sales Solutions:

711 West Gordon Terrace, Suite 106 . Chicago, Illinois 60613   Phone: 773.755.1306   Fax: 773.442.0840
www.toddnatenberg.com   e-mail todd@toddnatenberg.com

PERSONAL PROFILE
Todd B. Natenberg
President
TBN Sales Solutions
711 W. Gordon Terrace, Ste. 106, Chicago, IL 60613
Phone: (773) 755-1306, Fax: (773) 442-0840
todd@toddnatenberg.com, www.toddnatenberg.com

As the president and founder of TBN Sales Solutions (TBNSS), Todd is responsible for the day-to-day operations of the company. His responsibilities include earning new clients as well as delivering customized sales training. Through the establishment of universal structures in all facets of the sales processes, Todd increases sales commissions and dramatically improves the retention rates of sales employees.

Prior to the formation of TBNSS, Todd was a sales manager and regional sales trainer for Teligent, Inc. in Chicago, a full-service integrated provider offering local, long distance and data services nationwide.

As the company's first Midwest Regional Sales Trainer, Todd taught sales teams in Chicago, Denver, Milwaukee and Cleveland. He conducted new hire training and wrote Teligent's first sales presentation.

Todd's telecommunications career dates back to 1996 where he began with LCI International and was one of the top reps in Chicago. Prior to Teligent, he worked at USN Communications, a local reseller, where he achieved top sales success and was a part-time trainer. Previously, he sold photocopiers and fax machines.

A graduate of the University of Missouri-Columbia School of Journalism, Todd also was a newspaper reporter in suburban Chicago and freelanced for various publications, including the *Chicago Tribune.* He still contributes regularly to various sales magazines.

His latest book, *"I just got a job in sales. Now what?" A Playbook for Skyrocketing Commissions,* was released in 2003. Todd's first book, *The Journey Within: Two Months on Kibbutz,* was published in 2002 by Iuniverse.

711 West Gordon Terrace, Suite 106 . Chicago, Illinois 60613   Phone: 773.755.1306   Fax: 773.442.0840
www.toddnatenberg.com   e-mail todd@toddnatenberg.com

PERSONAL PROFILE (CONT.)

PROFESSIONAL EXPERIENCE

AT&T Inc..
Chicago, IL
Voice Account Executive

Teligent, Inc.
Chicago, IL
Regional Sales Trainer/Sales Manager

USN Communications
Schaumburg, IL
Sr. Sales Rep/Certified Tutor

Canon/Ambassador Office Equipment
Chicago, IL
Sales Rep., Business Systems Division

LCI International
Rosemont, IL
Account Executive I/II

The Arizona Republic
Phoenix, AZ
*Pulliam Fellowship/State
Government Reporter*

Daily Herald
Arlington Heights, IL
Staff writer

PROFESSIONAL ORGANIZATIONS

National Speakers Association-Illinois Chapter
Society of Professional Journalists
Former Chicago Big Brother
Former Arlington Heights Youth Commissioner
Chicagoland Chamber of Commerce

PHILOSOPHY

*"Customers do not care how much you know until they know how much
you care."*

"Sell how you want to buy."

What TBN SALES SOLUTIONS Can Do For You

TBN Sales Solutions increases commissions for salespeople and profits for companies through customized training, coaching and consultations.

We establish structures and procedures in all facets of the sales processes, through classroom workshops and individual sales coaching, to teach reps to take ownership of their businesses, thereby impacting the bottom line.

TBN programs range from 5 days to 1/2-day:

- Goal Setting and Time Management
- Prospecting
- Running a Sales Call
- Objection Handling
- Networking
- Team Building (includes personality profiles)
- Leadership
- Maintenance

In addition, TBN develops customized sales tools and provides consultative services in the following:

- Written Assessments/Recommendations
- Ride Alongs
- Individual Sales Coaching

ALL TBN Services include:

- *FREE* monthly subscription to *Skyrocketing Sales Solutions!*
- *FREE* advertisement on www.toddnatenberg.com
- *FREE* access to Todd's network (#'s some 10,000 contacts)

TBN brings a unique approach to the sales training process. Combining humor with personal and professional stories, Todd uses all facets to teach the art of selling. A "facilitator," his programs are interactive and entertaining. From Hollywood movies to articles, to traditional role plays, nothing is out of bounds for Todd to reinforce his proven sales beliefs.

For more information about TBN Sales Solutions, please call Todd Natenberg, president, at (773) 755-1306. He also can be reached at todd@toddnatenberg.com. Please visit www.toddnatenberg.com to learn more.

WHAT THEY SAY ABOUT TBN SALES SOLUTIONS

"I've signed new contracts and brought on new clients over the last three months using your techniques and ideas. My overall approach to sales is more structured and effective after having your sales coaching. I would highly recommend you to anyone wishing to get a better understanding of the sales process or to refine their marketing and sales strategy. I have a much, much better grasp of the sales process and how to use it."

Nathan Laurell, Partner, Technacity, LLC, Chicago, IL

"Since participating in your Prospecting, Time Management and Goal Setting seminars less than a month ago, we have had a record month in sales. The simple but powerful tools we have learned have helped us gain a new momentum and will give us the confidence to maintain it."

Alex Puig, CEO, Allied Computer Training Centers

"To say everyone was a little dubious at first is to say it mildly, but your enthusiasm and ability to motivate people is really impressive. The feedback we have gotten from the salespeople has been nothing but spectacular. I really feel that deep down your programs are going to increase sales for Wadsworth and for the salesmen. It becomes a win-win situation for everyone."

Dave Reed, VP of Sales, Wadsworth Pumps

"Your training was extremely beneficial and we have seen immediate results. Our new salespeople are scheduling twice as much activity as the initial results from some of our other training classes. Much of this success is a direct result of your hands-on approach."

Paul Rosen, Vice President of Sales and Marketing, E-Chx, Inc.

"I just had a staff meeting, and sure enough, a large percentage of the staff are still using the time management techniques you presented at our corporate offsite. I appreciated your presentation techniques and I know the majority of the staff found your presentations entertaining and informative."

Mark Cleaver, CEO, Technomic International

"I can't tell you how energized our people were as a result of your program. You certainly exceeded my expectations, which as you know, were extremely high from the beginning. I certainly look forward to working with you in the future. Your passion, energy and commitment to helping people grow is inspiring."

Leslie Smigel, Property Manager, Shorewood Properties

Three documents worth highlighting are "Personal Profile," "What (Your Company) Can Do for You" and "Testimonials."

- *Personal Profile*

Although you work for a great company, *you* are the product you are selling. Personalize your sale. Prospects like it when salespeople share their interests and previous employment history. Include your background, in the industry and outside the industry. If you are new to the industry, your "greenness" can mean you are more dedicated to helping others, because you do not yet have many customers to help. If you have been around for a while, your experience becomes your trademark.

Include sales awards if you've received any at your company. People love working with top reps.

Keep it two pages.

- *What (Your Company) Can Do for You*

In addition to marketing brochures, include a one-page promotional sheet printed on your company letterhead. (Your boss will appreciate it, too, because it's inexpensive to produce.) It's personal and presents a good overview for the prospect. Brochures typically demonstrate features, but this will show benefits. Include your contact information. This tool also can be used as an "On-The-Spot Thank You Letter" at the end of the sales call. Here's suggested wording:

> "Prospect So-and-So, I know we talked about a lot of information. Here's a one-page summary of what we discussed. My customers find it useful. Perhaps this will help you understand how we can help, in a nutshell."

- *Testimonials*

People love to hear others say good things about people they do business with. They don't only want to hear good things about the company. They want to know what kind of person you are. Ask all your customers for testimonial letters. Here's how to ask:

    – Ask them to address the letter to your boss

    – Don't have them write "To Whom It May Concern"

    – Don't write the letter for them

Here's suggested words to use requesting testimonials:

> "Customer So-and-So, I need your help. Could you write me a testimonial letter? I don't want to write it for you. If you think I don't deserve it, then please don't write it. But if you do, what I'd like is for you to address it to my boss and endorse three aspects: me, this product and my company. That would be great."

Besides being visual aids for your prospects, these written materials become resources for you.

As a salesperson, your technical knowledge will be limited. It's okay if you have to check with company specialists for this type of information. Prospects recognize this. However, they do expect you to have certain information about your company and general product and pricing knowledge stored in your memory or at least readily accessible. That's why it's critical you have your handy site-seller with you at all times.

The following page is a "cheat sheet" of everything you should know about your company and your products. Adjust it accordingly. At some point in your career, you may be asked everything on this list. You'd be amazed how curious prospects can be. If you think some of the questions are too personal, such as questions about your compensation package, then politely refuse to answer. But know the answers, just in case.

What Prospects Might Ask

General Company

- How old is your company?
- What year was it founded? Incorporated?
- Where was it founded? Incorporated?
- Corporate headquarters? Regional headquarters?
- How many offices nationwide? Statewide? Internationally?
- Are you public? Which exchange is the stock traded? Symbol? Today's value?
- How many employees nationwide? Statewide? International? Total?
- How many salespeople nationwide? Statewide? International? Total?
- How are your divisions arranged? Who do you target? What areas do you target?
- Who is on the executive board? Who is the CEO/CFO/VP of sales?
- What is the mission statement?
- What is the website?
- Who does the company sponsor? Charities? Community Service?
- Where do you advertise?
- What are the contact numbers and e-mails of the sales manager, regional vice president of sales, director of sales and customer service?
- What were revenues last year? Last quarter?
- What were revenues two years ago?
- Who are the biggest customers?
- What is the key to the company's success?
- What is the biggest challenge for you? For your company?
- Recent press releases? Recent media about your company?
- What else does the company sell outside of your division?
- What are your company's long-term plans? Revenue? Expansion? Products?

Your Product

- How much does it cost? How much does each item cost?
- Package deal? Price good for how long?
- Month to month/1 year/2 year/3 year commitment?
- Monthly/quarterly/annual commitment? Gross? Net?
- How long does it take to get it up and running? Delivered?

continued on next page

What Prospects Might Ask (cont.)

Your Product (cont.)

- Do I have to be there for delivery of your service? Will installation of your service interrupt my current service? If so, for how long?
- Procedure for delivery?
- 24-hour customer service? Online?
- Who do I call if there is a problem initially? 1 month? 6 months?
- Price guarantee? 30-day window? 90-day window to cancel?
- Payment is due before delivery? 30 days of delivery?
- 1-year layaway plan?
- How do the bills come? Paper? CD? On line? Automatic check/credit card?
- Does someone review my bill? Do you review my bill?
- Automatic renewal of agreement? You call me 1-month prior?
- What do I sign? Do I get a copy of it?
- What are the internal documents you hand in?
- Sample bill? Sample product?
- Instruction manual?

Employee

- How long have you been with your company?
- Why did you take the job?
- Where do you rank among the salespeople at your company?
- What has been the key to your success?
- Have you won any awards?
- Do you have any letters of recommendation? References?
- Hobbies?
- Long-term goals?
- What city do you live in? Family? Local organizations?
- What certification do you have?
- Are you involved in the community?
- How do you know So-and-So who referred you to me?

Now that we know what we are going to say, *how* are we going to say it? Even though you are not a public speaker, to succeed in sales you need to speak well. Don't worry. If you weren't able to articulate well, you wouldn't have made it this far.

Be emotional

If you are a shy and quiet person, pretend you're not! You are in sales. You need to be excited about your product in order for others to be. If you don't believe in your product, who else will?

Mirror speech patterns of your prospect

As we discussed earlier, mimic your prospect as much as possible. While you need to be emotional and passionate, if the prospect is an analytical, slow talker, don't display an overwhelming energy level. Be enthusiastic, but in a different way. Instead of talking fast, use gestures and smile.

Keep It Simple, Stupid

Even the most technical person wants a simple presentation. If you confuse the prospect, the sale is over. Don't make the prospect work. It's another recurring theme – simplicity.

The simpler the sales process, the quicker the sell. The simpler the product, the quicker the sell. No one wants something simpler than the complex person.

Interact

It may be your turn to talk, but you must include your prospect in the presentation. To ensure that prospects are listening, engage them in the discussion. Check that they are acknowledging, repeating and taking action based on what you say. Some great ways to interact without losing control include:

- Making eye contact with prospects
- Asking "What do you think so far?"
- Placing handouts directly in front of prospects

When prospects can see and feel your presentation, they connect more with you and your product. This touches their own emotions, an essential element of the buying process.

Tie back the alignments you created probing

You spent lots of time asking great questions. Use the information. Whenever possible, reference the past conversation. It proves you listened. Build those alliances. You might say, "Like you told me earlier about your company's success being based on great customer service, the same can be said for our company."

Trial close

Trial closing is the strongest way to interact with prospects. It's also a great way to ultimately close the deal. Trial closing involves gathering prospects' buy-in along the way. Encourage "yes" to be their only response at the end, because they've been busy "yesing" along the way. Trial closes enable deals to close themselves. The following are good questions to ask at the appropriate times:

- "How will this help you?"
- "How much money will that save you?"
- "How much time will that save you?"
- "How many more hours a day will that give you?"
- "How will that help employee morale?"

Closing a sale is like an algebra formula. If A=B and B=C, then A=C. If the prospect agrees with A and A=yes, and the prospect agrees with C and C=yes, then yes=yes.

Transitions/Stay on track

Don't turn the presentation into a one-way conversation, but do stay on track. Transitions are helpful. Address prospects' comments and questions as you go, but stay focused. If a prospect wants to know the price, there is nothing wrong with saying, "We will get to that in a moment. Bear with me." If the prospect gets impatient, give a quick answer and return to your topic. Likewise, if the prospect seems bored by your presentation, address it. Don't wait until the end. Your instincts are probably correct.

Never talk about price until the very end

Once the prospect appears to be on-board, summarize again the benefits of what you outlined. Then ask for questions. If prospects say they understand, now it's time to discuss the "investment opportunity you are inviting your prospect to participate in."

The key to addressing price successfully is to be matter-of-fact. If you have done your job properly, the prospect should be so excited that price is irrelevant.

Expensive is only expensive if it does not satisfy a need. There is price and then there is cost. Sell cost.

If the prospect wants to buy, stop talking!

Don't talk yourself out of a deal. If all goes as planned, the prospect will cut you off and sign the deal right there. Does this always happen? Of course not. But sometimes when prospects are ready to buy, salespeople insist on finishing their presentations. They finish their presentations, but they frequently lose the deal.

Resummarize at the end

You have presented a lot of great information. You have spoken well. All information is important, but people remember most what they hear last. Don't expect the prospect to remember everything you've said. Simplify it. Here's how:

> "So Prospect So-and-So, our programs will address all your needs: customer service, billing and the overall quality of what you are looking for. These were all things you mentioned that were important to you. Do you have any questions?"

Let's take a moment to examine a different kind of appointment, one known as the "proposal appointment." Ideally, you skip over this unneeded delay in the sales process. In essence, your presentation should constitute your proposal. However, due to some poor selling habits of others, some prospects have become accustomed to requesting salespeople to put together written recommendations. They then require salespeople to present these recommendations in a separate meeting. Honor their request, but be wary.

A proposal is nothing more than a written explanation of what you are recommending to solve a prospect's problem.

A proposal appointment only differs from a first appointment by the addition of a few necessary steps. If you are required to write a proposal, what should you include? How should you react to the prospect?

First, clarify why prospects want a proposal and define what they consider a proposal. Say this:

"Every prospect is unique with unique needs. What would you like me to put in my proposal for you and your company? What do you want to see?"

Prospects usually ask for proposals just because other salespeople have presented them with this information. Don't fall into the same poor selling habits. To understand an effective proposal, let's explore what proposals are and what they are not.

Proposals are not:

- Price quotes

- Documents automatically written just because prospects ask for them

- Price leveraging by prospects to garner a lower price from a competitor, including the current vendor

Proposals will vary based on your company and your industry. But here's an overview of what to include:

- Cover page including date, attention information and company logo of the prospect's company

- Table of contents

- A written summary of your proposed solution

- A "What (My Company) Can Do For You" letter

- Your profile

- Contacts at your company

- Letters of recommendation (if you have them)

- Pricing for each facet of the proposal

- Contacts/Agreements to sign at the end

- Printout of e-mails (prospects like summaries and organization)

As you may have noticed, almost all the items you have with you right in your "site-seller." The goal of proposing a solution is nothing short of closing the deal.

Close

There is no easier step in the sales process, but there is no scarier step. What's the worst that can happen? The prospect says no? No, the worst scenario is that the prospect wants to "think about it."

In our every day personal lives, don't most of us want "closure" – good or bad? Uncertainty drives us crazy. Selling is no different. The good news is that if you have followed the process properly and you have made it to this point, the odds are greatly in your favor.

How do we close? Many books have been written on the subject. Indeed, many have been written, as well, about how not to close. Let's focus here on proper ways, rather than the improper. Don't beat around the bush. Just be direct.

Here's suggested wording:

> "So Prospect So-and-So, that's how it works. What do you think?"

> "So Prospect So-and-So, it sounds good to me. Would you like to try us out?"

> "So Prospect So-and-So, what do you think? Should we process the paperwork?"

> "So Prospect So-and-So, when should we schedule delivery?"

> "So Prospect So-and-So, all I need is your signature right here and we'll get you going."

The key components to closing are:

- Unshakable confidence

You must believe that if you were on the other side of the table, you would buy your services – right then and there. One reason some reps have a tough time closing is because of their own buying habits. You cannot ask someone for an order and expect them to purchase if you really know that you would not buy at that moment. If *you* would not purchase your own product at that moment if you were sitting on the other side of the table, you will be unable to ask your prospect for the order. Prospects can sense if you don't believe in what you are offering. They will tell themselves, "If the salesperson doesn't think I should buy, then I probably shouldn't."

- Silence

Ask and be as quiet as a mouse. If you speak, you could blow the deal. Don't interrupt the prospect's train of thought. Silence is deafening, but it's a very powerful tool. Silence means prospects are thinking. It means they are thinking about *why* to buy your services. They are justifying the purchase in their minds.

- Preparation

Have paperwork filled out ahead of time. It shows your organizational skills and your confidence. Remember the importance of simplicity. The easier it is to buy, the greater the likelihood they will.

Here is another type of close. Do what works best for you.

> "I'll tell you what. It sounds like there might be an opportunity here for us to help. Since we are both here now, why don't we sign the paperwork? I will call you in two days. If you decide against it, I will rip up the paperwork. This way, though, we can work by phone. You know integrity is everything to me. If I turned in an order without your authorization, I'd be fired. "

This close often works, but you must be comfortable with it. It's not for everyone. I've used it many times in my career and often prospects have signed. Statistically, when I've called back two days later, 90% of the time there are no problems. There have been times when prospects have said "rip it up." I have, and our relationships are all the stronger.

This close is recommended, because it gives you a measure of the level of the prospects' real interest. When prospects say, "It sounds great. I know we're going to do it. Just give me a couple days," sometimes the prospect is not being completely open. Sometimes the prospect is outright lying.

Try this close once and see what happens.

Not recommended

"Our price will increase in a week (a month)."

This is a very negative close. Be careful with it. There are companies that use it effectively and legitimately. After all, most buyers don't question retail stores that have sales for a "limited time."

The key is to publicize when the price will increase. If you choose to play the "If you don't buy now, it will go up tomorrow" game, you'd better be telling the truth. Even if you close the deal, there could be bad blood. It'd be a shame to ruin your credibility and professionalism with something so trivial.

Of all the critical components of closing, none is more important than being prepared to walk away. You will not sell everyone all the time. You can only do so much. We discussed earlier how you will never sell 1/3 of your opportunities no matter what you do. As we discovered earlier, he worst thing that can happen on a sale is not that the prospect says "no." A "no" at least provides closure.

It's the "I don't knows" that are most troubling. The problem with "I don't know" is that since the prospect doesn't know, neither do you.

In these cases, one of the best strategies is to challenge. Challenge hard. You don't want to upset the prospect because often a sale occurs one, two, three months, or even a year later. However, you don't want to spin your wheels unnecessarily. By challenging, you will find out where you truly stand.

A good, non-threatening way to measure a prospect's level of interest after an "I don't know" comment is to request a commitment to another appointment to sign the paperwork. If the prospect agrees, let go of the idea of closing the sale at that moment. You have done your job. You can leave feeling comfortable that you stand a good chance to get the deal at the next meeting.

If the prospect won't sign and won't commit to a timeframe, try a different tactic. With unshakable confidence, say:

> "Prospect So-and-So. Let me ask you upfront.
> I know when I'm not interested in something,
> I say the same thing: 'I'm not sure. Call me
> next week.' If that's what you are saying, I
> respect that and we can part friends. But I
> don't want to waste your time or mine. They
> are equally valuable. Is that what you are
> telling me?"

The answer might be, "Yes, that's what I'm saying." If it is, congratulations. You now know to move on. But most times, prospects will defend themselves. "No, I just need more time. I really am interested. Honest."

So what did we learn about running a sales call? The steps are:

1. Prepare.
2. Send PAL (Purpose/Agenda/Limit).
3. Introduce to gatekeeper.
4. Research while waiting.
5. Set the agenda.
6. Reposition.
7. Probe.
8. Summarize.
9. Present.
10. Close.

Sell how you want to buy.

CHAPTER 7

Follow-up

Follow-up: The many steps via phone, fax and e-mail that are performed after an initial contact with an individual or company in an effort to earn new clients

Selling is putting yourself in the right place at the right time to satisfy the right needs. Hard work is often disguised as good luck.

It is rare for buyers to contact salespeople to explicitly say they need their services. "Need" is a relative word. There are only three things humans truly need: food, shelter and water. Everything else is a "want." Does a company really *need* better phone service? Does a Controller really *need* to purchase new office equipment? Do CEOs *need* to impact the bottom line of their organizations?

So when buyers tell salespeople, "We will call you if we need you," they are usually saying they aren't interested. Even when they determine they do need your services, they still may not call.

When a contract with their current vendor expires, buyers *need* a certain service. Indeed, they may even be unhappy with their current vendor and want to hire another vendor. But will they call you? How companies determine which organizations they need is often based on one factor – follow-up.

Follow-up earned me the business of one of my very first clients. The opportunity arose when my prospect, Matt, told me in June to call him "around the holidays," knowing his agreement with his current provider would expire at that time. I called, and as a result, he bought my services.

"I'm just curious, Matt," I commented as he signed the paperwork. "Your agreement with the current vendor was due to expire, but if I hadn't contacted you, would you have contacted me? After all, you said you were interested and there was a need."

"Absolutely not," Matt answered. "Had you not called me, I would have just renewed our current agreement."

"Even though ours was clearly a better deal?" I asked.

"Yes, Todd," Matt said. "What earned you this deal was you knew the difference between persistence and insistence."

In this chapter, we will discuss the procedure for following up sales calls:

1. E-mail everyone a thank you letter within two days.

2. Confirm/Acknowledge commitments.

4. Summarize meeting.

5. Update regularly.

6. Refer business to prospect.

7. Send monthly newsletter.

E-mail everyone a thank you letter within two days

Handwritten thank you letters used to be special. They showed that salespeople took a personal interest in their customers. Unfortunately, handwritten notes do two other things as well: They show messy handwriting and they do not reach as many people at one time as e-mail.

In this day and age, most people prefer e-mail. When you e-mail information to people who actually want to correspond with you, it simplifies your life – and theirs. We've all spoken with people who say, "I know I have that information some-where. Let me check my e-mail."

Thank anyone you meet in a formal appointment, networking event or informal conversation via e-mail. Don't limit e-mail to those who need your services right now. Add *everyone* to your database. Often sending thank you letters to prospects who say "no" may get you the deal in the end simply because you were the only one to follow-up. Also, remember the power of referrals. Even though a prospect may not directly be a candidate for your services, they may know someone who could benefit from meeting you.

The reason for sending e-mail two days after your meeting is that the two-day timeframe reinforces your message at a time when it needs reinforcing. This may go against conventional thinking, but let's explore the reasons.

When salespeople meet with prospects, the two parties exchange much information. Even on perfectly conducted sales calls where simplicity is the cornerstone, it's rare for a deal to close at the initial meeting. Prospects often must consider your information and analyze it on their own after the appointment. They are overwhelmed upon the conclusion of the meeting, although they are interested. They need to digest your informa-tion. Frequently, prospects won't even look at your materials for at least a day. If you send e-mail the day of the meeting, they may not read it. If they do read it, they will commend you for your follow-up, but what you say in the e-mail may go in one ear and out the other.

But, after a few days, prospects are happy to be reminded of what they know they wanted to examine. They can see if their interpretation of the meeting matches up with yours. It's the difference between "persistent" and "insistent," to quote customer Matt.

Confirm/Acknowledge commitments

E-mail holds everyone accountable. It ensures that you and prospects are on the same page. Remember how real things become when they are written down? By confirming and summarizing your conversations about the prospect's needs, your recommended solution and how the two connect, you advance the sale. In your e-mail, spell out the next step you and the prospect will take together. If you have a follow-up appointment, reference it. If you do not, but you have a timeframe, reference that. If there is no interest and it's a "down the road" situation, confirm it. Personalize the letter.

Summarize the meeting

Prove you listened. Remind prospects of their needs and how you offered to help. Include a written solution or your electronic brochure even if they already have the hard copy. This memory-jogger helps you, but it also helps your prospect remember the benefits you offer.

It's easier to forward e-mailed information than hard copy. Of course, you will review your materials in-person but adding electronic versions "for your convenience" is a nice touch. Prospects will be thankful they don't have to ask themselves, "Where did I put that information?"

The following pages include sample follow-up letters "for your convenience." The letters differ depending on the type of meeting and the result of the meeting.

First Appointment Thank You Letter

Subject: Skyrocketing sales for XXX – Todd Natenberg, TBN Sales Solutions President, says thanks for meeting with me

So-and-So,

Thanks very much for meeting with me last week to discuss ways to skyrocket sales for XXX. I appreciate the consideration.

Per our conversation and my previous discussion with John Smith of company XYZ who originally referred me to you, I am confident that after your evaluation you will agree we offer the best programs in today's sales training industry.

I am looking forward to our next scheduled appointment on January 10 at 2 p.m.

Our proposed solution will demonstrate further how we will help specifically with those key areas we discussed where you want assistance: cold calling, objection handling and an overall sales process for your organization. TBN's customized approach will enable your salespeople to regain the focus you indicated they now lack. It will give them the confidence you indicated that is so vital to their success.

To reiterate, TBN Sales Solutions increases commissions for salespeople and profits for businesses through customized training, coaching and consulting. By establishing structures and procedures for organizations, through classroom workshops and individual sales coaching, we teach employees to take ownership of their business, to impact the bottom line.

Please call (773) 755-1306 or e-mail todd@toddnatenberg.com with questions. Thanks again for the consideration.

I look forward to seeing you on January 10 at 2 p.m.

Sincerely,
Todd Natenberg
President

TBN Sales Solutions
711 W. Gordon Terrace, Ste. 106 Chicago, IL 60613
Phone: 773-755-1306, Fax: 773-442-0840, Outside Chicago: 866-464-0339
e-mail: todd@toddnatenberg.com http://www.toddnatenberg.com

TBN Sales Solutions increases commissions for salespeople and profits for businesses through customized training, coaching and consulting. We establish structures and procedures in all facets of the sales process, through classroom workshops and individual sales coaching, to teach reps to control their own destinies, to impact the bottom line.

Second Appointment Thank You Letter

Subject: Skyrocketing sales for XXX – Todd Natenberg, TBN Sales Solutions President, says thanks again for meeting with me

So-and-So,

I just wanted to drop you a quick note to say thanks again for chatting with me about a potential partnership between XXX and TBN Sales Solutions. I'm excited to work with your salespeople to start increasing commissions.

Per our conversation, I'm looking forward to meeting with you next on Jan. 20 at 2 p.m. At that time – if all is a go – we will sign the necessary paperwork and schedule dates for training.

I also have enclosed our solution electronically for your convenience. I thought you'd find it helpful.

Please call (773) 755-1306 or e-mail todd@toddnatenberg.com with questions. Thanks again for the consideration.

I look forward to seeing you on January 20 at 2 p.m.

Sincerely,
Todd Natenberg
President

TBN Sales Solutions
711 W. Gordon Terrace, Ste. 106
Chicago, IL 60613
Phone: 773-755-1306, Fax: 773-442-0840, Outside Chicago: 866-464-0339
e-mail: todd@toddnatenberg.com
http://www.toddnatenberg.com

TBN Sales Solutions increases commissions for salespeople and profits for businesses through customized training, coaching and consulting. We establish structures and procedures in all facets of the sales process, through classroom workshops and individual sales coaching, to teach reps to control their own destinies, to impact the bottom line.

Undecided/No Interest Thank You Letter

Subject: Skyrocketing sales for XXX – Todd Natenberg, TBN Sales Solutions President, says thanks for meeting with me

So-and-So,

Thanks very much for meeting with me last week to discuss ways to skyrocket sales for XXX. I appreciate the consideration.

Per our conversation, and my previous discussion with John Smith of Company XYZ who originally referred me to you, I am confident that after your evaluation you will agree we offer the best programs in today's sales training industry.

Naturally, I'm disappointed there is not more of an immediate opportunity to help. However, one thing I have learned in business is that what is not an opportunity today could always be one tomorrow. All I ask is that should your situation change, you will keep TBN Sales Solutions in mind.

Per your request, I will follow-up with you in two months. In the interim, should anything change, please keep me posted.

To reiterate, TBN Sales Solutions increases commissions for salespeople and profits for businesses through customized training, coaching and consulting. We establish structures and procedures in all facets of the sales process, through classroom workshops and individual sales coaching, to teach reps to control their own destinies, to impact the bottom line.

Also, should you hear of any companies looking for top-notch sales training, please feel free to pass along my name and materials. You always can reach me at (773) 755-1306 or todd@toddnatenberg.com. I appreciate the help.

Thanks again for the consideration. I look forward to speaking with you in two months.

Sincerely,
Todd Natenberg
President

TBN Sales Solutions
711 W. Gordon Terrace, Ste. 106 Chicago, IL 60613
Phone: 773-755-1306, Fax: 773-442-0840, Outside Chicago: 866-464-0339
e-mail: todd@toddnatenberg.com http://www.toddnatenberg.com

TBN Sales Solutions increases commissions for salespeople and profits for businesses through customized training, coaching and consulting. We establish structures and procedures in all facets of the sales process, through classroom workshops and individual sales coaching, to teach reps to control their own destinies, to impact the bottom line.

Update regularly

Organizing yourself in the follow-up process is critical to success. Just because prospects aren't interested today, this doesn't mean they won't be interested tomorrow. But if salespeople don't update prospects on a regular basis, they can miss out. Have a system for updating. Include the following:

- Schedule the date and time to follow-up in your datebook.

- Treat updating as an appointment. Stick to it.

- Never follow-up on a cell phone. (The phone sounds awful and you can't take notes.)

- Leave voice mail if the person you are trying to reach is not in.

We discussed earlier the importance of leaving messages to give prospects reasons to call you back. Now leave messages to alert prospects you are the one calling back. In other words, when prospects tell you to follow-up with them on a certain day or month, let them know you are honoring that commitment. You'd be amazed at how many prospects are aware who follows-up and who doesn't.

Just because you can't reach prospects doesn't mean they aren't interested. Here's a recommended message to leave:

> "Hello, Prospect So-and-So. This is Todd Natenberg, TBN Sales Solutions, (773) 755-1306. Sorry I missed you. I promised I'd follow-up with you today and I always follow through on my commitments. I just wanted to check in to see where we are. Please call me. Again, it's Todd Natenberg (773) 755-1306. Thanks very much."

Other ways to update regularly include:

- Sending new articles about your industry or their industry via fax or e-mail

- Sending information about your company launching a new product, promotion or program

The key is you need a reason to update. Talk about something new – anything. Don't just call to say, "Want to buy?"

Refer business to prospects

We will talk more about this in the Networking chapter, but one of the best ways to earn business is to refer business. Even if nothing comes of it, prospects appreciate that you were thinking about helping them even before they paid you money for your services. Referrals mean you want to develop relationships – not close deals. When you refer business, do it via e-mail. You will certainly want to keep a record of this.

Don't limit your referrals to potential clients for your potential clients. For instance, if you know someone who provides a service or product you think can help one of your prospects, refer that person. Remember, everyone benefits with referrals.

Send a monthly newsletter

If people continually complain they are repeatedly bombarded with promotions and other forms of e-mail marketing, then why do electronic newsletters still exist? It's because they work.

If you or your company can afford one, a hard copy newsletter is very effective, but only as an addition to the electronic version. "E-zines," as they are called, are productive because they are convenient. They don't take up paper space and readers can forward the material to others. In addition, they facilitate record-keeping.

To make the most out of your electronic newsletter, it must be valuable to prospects. Give *free* information relevant to your product and industry that – if utilized – will impact the bottom line for your prospects. This does two things: keeps your name in front of the prospect and further establishes you, the sales-person, as an asset.

Decide what to include in your newsletter. Content will vary depending on your industry and your style. But a few recommendations are:

• Industry articles to keep prospects up to date on the latest and greatest in your field

• Articles about your company or product specifically that appear in other publications (or perhaps your own internal newsletter)

• A "tip" of the month relevant to what you do

• New promotions or products at your company

The best place to acquire these materials is by subscribing to electronic newsletters. Why not? There's no charge. In addition, sending these articles are very easy utilizing "cut and paste" features.

At TBN Sales Solutions, we utilize a service called Constant Contact that provides templates for various links. Here's what our newsletter, *Skyrocketing Sales Solutions!*, entails:

• Sales Tip of the Month (an article highlighting a proven sales technique)

• Buying Star of the Month (an article highlighting a situation where we witnessed top notch sales skills while we participated as buyers)

- Where's TBN Sales Solutions? (a description of recent media coverage or happenings at our company)

- Networking Star of the Month (referrals and links to a company of our choosing in a different industry whose products we are recommending)

- Contact information for TBN Sales Solutions

- The ability to forward the newsletter

- The ability to be "removed" from the mailing list

Our newsletter also enables us to "cut and paste" photos and graphics.

To reiterate, the steps to follow-up are these:

1. **E-mail everyone a thank you letter within two days.**

2. **Confirm/Acknowledge commitments.**

4. **Summarize meeting.**

5. **Update regularly.**

6. **Refer business to prospect.**

7. **Send monthly newsletter.**

Selling is about how many times you can get in front of how many opportunities in how many ways to communicate valuable information.

Overcome Objections

*If a concern by a prospect can't be overcome by you or
another vendor, it is not an objection.*

Peole buy on emotion. Think of your own buying habits.
When was the last time you made a significant purchase
and did not ask a single question? When was the last time
you bought, but did not voice any concerns? Take it one step
further. When was the last time you were uninterested in an
item, but asked questions about it? People only have concerns
if they are interested … if there is something about which to be
concerned.

I recently bought a two-bedroom condominium. Prior to
purchasing, I examined other potential properties. I asked no
questions about the ones in which I had no interest. These
homes were usually out of my price range, did not meet my
geographical needs or were not the size I wanted. There was no
point in discussing these matters because nothing could be
done about most of these issues. They were what they were.

But prior to taking out a mortgage on the home I was interested in, I asked many questions. "How much are assess-
ments?" "Where will I park?" "Is it a good neighborhood?" "Is
there extra storage?" "Parking will cost how much per month?"

My realtor helped me overcome these objections by tapping
into my emotions. But he was only able to tap in because I let
him. He was only able to because I told him what I was worried
about. One by one, we addressed each of my concerns. One by
one, we converted my fear into excitement.

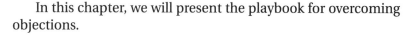

In this chapter, we will present the playbook for overcoming objections.

1. Pause.

2. Relax.

3. Empathize.

4. Probe.

5. Playback.

6. Avoid self-imposed objections.

7. Solve.

Pause

When a prospect expresses a concern, do nothing. Don't respond – initially. Recognize that what was spoken is still only a concern. It's not yet an objection. Maybe the prospect is thinking out loud. The prospect could be talking for the sake of talking. You don't know what is going through the prospect's mind. How often have you blurted out comments with no intention of getting a response?

Don't interrupt your prospect's thought process. Thinking takes work. Having to think again takes even more work. One of the best ways to simplify the sales process for prospects is to give them time to think. Their silence means they are thinking about why to buy your service, not why not to buy. If they did not want to buy, they'd just say so.

Compare selling with the role of parents watching their child fall down. Have you seen children who fall, but don't cry right away? They look for the reaction of their parents. If their parents say nothing, often the child moves on. But if the parent rushes over, worried and concerned, tears inevitably flow. Children's reactions as to whether their pain is justified is often determined by the validation their parents do or don't give. The world of sales is no different. In my telecommunications days, more than one conversation like the following occurred:

Prospect:	"It sounds good, Todd. But six cents a minute is more than I was hoping to pay."
Me:	*Silence*
Me:	*Silence*
Prospect:	"But I guess it's a good price. I'm still saving money. Let's do it."

There is another reason to pause. Gather your own thoughts. Digest what was said. Think before you speak. What you eventually say will be crucial.

Relax

Take a deep breath. Count to ten. The silence you hear is an expression of emotion. If you relax, the prospect will, too. No one likes to argue with a wall.

The emotion of silence in response to a salesperson's statement is usually being expressed more in support of what you are offering than against.

Empathize

Now, you respond. You must say something before the prospect becomes annoyed. Don't argue, but don't validate the comment in its entirety at this point. Think of that parent's reaction to the child. Show you understand. Communicate to prospects that their concerns are valid, but not valid enough to not buy. In sales circles, this is known as "feel, felt, found." Here's the words to use:

"I understand how you feel, Prospect So-and-So. Other clients of ours have felt the same way. But what they have found after purchasing our services is that they made the right decision going with us."

Probe

If you still have not defused the situation with pause, relax and empathize, now you should ask questions to assess the situation. Make sure you understand what was spoken. What you think you heard and what the prospect intended are not always the same.

What, exactly, is the concern? What is the objection? Probing is important because it puts "concerns" into one of three categories: Statements, Deal-breakers and Objections.

Statements

Part of the definition of "objection" is that emotions must be expressed. A statement does not express emotions. Talking is not an emotion.

When you say "I don't know," that is not an emotion because you could mean "maybe" – or "maybe not." Indecisiveness is not an emotion. Happiness, sadness and anger are emotions. Make sense?

Deal-breaker

Ask yourself if your prospect's concern is one you can overcome. I've been in situations where a prospect has a 5-year contract with a $100,000 penalty if broken. My service would only save the prospect $1,000 overall. While stressing to never sell on price, a $100,000 penalty is a deal-breaker, unless I'm willing to make up the $99,000.

I moved on.

The challenge is determining whether something is truly a deal-breaker. What are the terms of the contract? Are there loopholes? Perhaps you could earn some of the business, but is it worth it?

Objection

How do we know when a concern is a legitimate objection? Certain criteria must be met.

- Emotion must be expressed – positive or negative.

- Specific, measurable issues must be voiced.

- The impact on the company's business must be real.

- There must be a clear solution – somewhere, somehow.

Overcoming objections is a form of negotiating. It is a win-win scenario. The goal is not to prove the prospect wrong. The goal is to have prospects prove themselves wrong. Lead prospects to overcome their own objections. Let them make their own decisions, with help from you.

Asking lots of questions, followed by long periods of silence, helps accomplish this task. Some good questions to ask include:

"How do you mean?"

"Oh, why is that?"

"I don't understand. Please help me out."

"Can you explain further? I'm confused."

At TBN Sales Solutions, we call this the "Columbo" theory. Years ago, *Columbo* was a popular television show starring Peter Falk as a bumbling detective. In the show, Columbo got

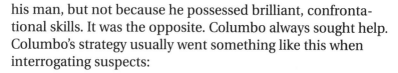
his man, but not because he possessed brilliant, confrontational skills. It was the opposite. Columbo always sought help. Columbo's strategy usually went something like this when interrogating suspects:

Columbo:	"I'm a little confused. Can you *help* me understand? Please say it again. It will *help* me out."
Suspect:	"Geez, Columbo. What don't you get? I killed the person. Understand?"
Columbo:	"Oh, I see ... You are under arrest."

Playback

When you have enough information to make a valid judgement as to whether this is a deal-breaker or an objection, repeat your understanding to the prospect. This does a few things:

• Ensures you and the prospect agree with what it is preventing you both from forging ahead

• Enables prospects to hear their own objections aloud

• Proves you were listening to the prospect

• If what you repeat does not match up with what the prospect meant to say, prospects will appreciate your desire to clarify

Here is an example.

You:	"Okay, Prospect So-and-So. I think I understand what you are saying. The issue for you is not that things are fine as they are. You are questioning whether it's worth the additional cost to have better customer service with us.

> You agree our service could – if executed properly – save your company 10 hours more per week, thereby impacting your bottom line greatly. But you question just how those 10 additional hours will come about.
>
> "In other words, you are not sure whether our overall value is worth it. If you were convinced that we really would save your company 10 hours per week, then we could go ahead. Is that right?

Prospect: "Yes."

You: "So the real issue is will our service do what we say?"

Prospect: "Yes, I guess that's the issue. Why don't you walk me through it again?"

Avoid self-imposed objections

We stated earlier that if you won't buy your own service, you can't sell it. The same theory is relevant to objections. If you think your price is too high, the prospect certainly will. Too often, salespeople think they know their company's limitations so well that they defend what does not need defending in the prospect's eyes.

For instance, if prospects say they are concerned about customer service, don't lower the price. They did not say the price was too high. You did. Not only is altering the price not necessary, it's counterproductive. Prospects may become angry that you did not listen to their true concerns. They may walk away for that reason alone. If they don't walk away, you may have cost yourself and your company money unnecessarily.

There is no easier way to lose a sale than to prove to prospects you did not listen to their concerns. Never address an objection the prospect does not want addressed.

One of the most common ways to self-impose objections is by being too technical. It's worth repeating: Keep It Simple. Consider again your own buying habits. If you are confused about something, how often will you ask for an explanation? If you are determined to buy an item at all costs, you will ask. But if you are on the bubble, more often than not you won't waste your time or energy. No one wants to look foolish.

Some salespeople defend being technical because they say that if prospects are confused, they will ask for clarification. But why make them work?

Make it easy for prospects to buy and they will. Make it hard, and they won't.

Solve

Solving an objection is similar to making your presentation, only abbreviated. To overcome the objection, utilize your visuals once again. The reason why is that when a true objection surfaces, prospects usually doubt what you said. They question the validity of your offering. Show them that what you said is fact, not opinion, by using support materials.

It's time for an exercise.

OVERCOMING OBJECTIONS EXERCISE

• Go into a room with open wall space.

• If you are on a sales team, gather your colleagues and manager to conduct this exercise with you.

• Gather 10 big pieces of paper – 11" x 24" is great, but 8.5" x 11" is fine, too.

• Tape each piece of paper to the wall.

• Label each piece of paper "Objections" #1-10.

• Brainstorm the top 10 objections you encounter in your daily job.

• Write each objection on each piece of paper.

• Write down every response you can think of.

The following pages list various suggested responses to common objections in the world of sales – regardless of industry. History has proven the effectiveness of these scripts. Remember to use these scripts only after pause, relax, empathize, probe and playback.

Objection handling scripts

"If it ain't broke don't fix it."

"I understand exactly how you feel. Several of my clients have felt the same way during our initial discussions. But what they have found after speaking with us is keeping things as they are does not always provide a solution that could grow their business. What we are talking about is a way to further impact your bottom line. What could the company do with this extra money? Isn't that a reason right there to improve the situation?"

"I need references."

"I don't mind giving you references, but before we do that, I want to make sure we have all our bases covered. Just like if you were my customer and I used you as a reference, I don't like bombarding my existing clients with phone calls from other opportunities until we have everything else ironed out. Is this the only thing standing between us and a new customer at this point?

"No? Then why don't we address the other issues first? Does that sound fair?"

"We don't have it in the budget."

You:	"How do you mean? Have it in the budget? Have what in the budget? Help me understand. I'm a little confused."
Prospect:	"Your price is too high. I can get your services for less down the street."

You:	"In what respect? My price? You mean you are worried you won't get the proper return on your investment? Help me out here."
Prospect:	"Yes, that's right – my return on the investment. I'm just not sure the change is worth it."
You:	"So the issue is not the price. You are questioning whether you will get the value you are looking for. You question whether we can deliver what we say? It's almost the 'too good to be true' situation?"
Prospect:	"Yeah, I guess that's it."
You:	"Well, let me explain our programs again."

"Your price is too high. I can get it for less somewhere else."

You:	"I'm a little confused. When we spoke earlier, you indicated what was important to you was reliability and one point of contact. You said those were the concerns of yours that were not being addressed by your current vendor. Did I miss something? Please clarify for me.
	"As I indicated earlier, we will never be the cheapest or the most expensive. Much like your business, we, too, have been successful because of our quality and service."

"Who are you? I've never heard of your company."

You:	"That's a fair question. I understand exactly how you feel. Several of my clients felt the same way during our initial discussions. But what they found out after speaking with us is

that because we are not one of the 'major players' we can provide unequaled personalized attention. Because we do not have as many customers as the larger companies, we must earn your business on a daily basis. That means I have to be head and shoulders above the rest. Much like your company, it's been the key to our success."

"We tried switching vendors before. It was a disaster. It's not worth the risk again."

You:	"You indicated that earlier, but it sounds like maybe we did not address it enough in depth. What specifically are you concerned would happen again? Help me understand. "
Prospect:	"The service went down. It cost us time and money and we had nothing to show for it."
You:	"So you question what we will do differently to ensure these problems don't repeat themselves?"
Prospect:	"Yes."
You: "	"Okay, so what you are saying is if you felt more comfortable that this would not happen, you'd be okay?"
Prospect:	"Yes."
You:	"I do understand how you feel. Several of my clients have felt the same way. What they have discovered – in the end – is that we delivered on our promises."
Prospect:	"Still, I'm just not sure. Why don't you walk me through it again?"

"We used your company before. It was a disaster."

You: "I am sorry to hear that. I offer no excuses. All I can ask you is if you had the opportunity to re-earn a customer's business you lost, wouldn't that be terrific?"

Prospect: "Sure it would."

You: "I do understand how you feel. Several other clients have felt the same way. What they have found out, after exploring our new services, is that we are a much better company now. In fact, it is because of those problems that my division was formed: to correct those problems we once made.

"It sounds good, but my boss will never go for this."

You (flinching, expression of surprise): "Your boss? I'm a little confused. When we spoke, you indicated you were the one who signed on the dotted line? I apologize if I misunderstood you."

Prospect: "Well, I just have to run it by him."

You (flinching again): "Okay. Well, if that's the case. I'll tell you what. Let's do a couple of things. Let's schedule an appointment with him, where you and I can position us together. What can you and I do to work as 'partners' to show him the benefits? If you were me, what would you recommend? Your ideas will really help me. "

Prospect: *(answers)*

You: "Also, naturally one question he will ask you is if you were him, what would you do?"

Prospect:	"Oh, if it were up to me I'd do it."
You:	"Terrific. Then my work is done – for the moment."

"We're bound by a contract."

You:	"How do you mean?"
Prospect:	"If we used you, we'd be penalized."
You:	"Forget us for a moment. What are the terms of the agreement? When does it expire? Would there be an opportunity for you to try out a portion of our services?"
Prospect:	"Yeah, I guess so – now that you mention it."

"There's no reason to do it now. Maybe later. I'll call you in two months."

You:	"Prospect So-and-So, we are both business people. I don't want to waste your time or my time. They are both equally valuable. I know when I'm not interested in something, that's exactly what I say. If you're saying you're not interested, I'll respect that and I'll move on. Am I reading you correctly?"
Prospect :	"No, not at all. I really am interested. It's just that later might be a better time. There's no rush."
You:	"All right. Then, let me ask you an upfront question. Why would another time be better than now? What would change that would create this sense of urgency?"
Prospect:	"I don't know. It's just we have a lot going on now. We don't have time to mess around with this."

You:	"Oh, I see. So you are concerned that switching to us would be the equivalent of 'messing around' and you are wondering what the repercussions would be if we did not deliver as promised?"
Prospect:	"Yes, I suppose so."
You:	"Well, in that case, let's review our programs again."
Prospect:	"No, just call me in two months."
You:	"Fair enough. The other thing I will tell you is that maybe our programs are not a good fit. That is possible. They are not for everybody. I'm confident we can help you, but in the end your decision will be based on your gut feeling. No fancy brochure or even proven history will alleviate that concern. Maybe we aren't what you looking for."
Prospect:	"Wait a second. I didn't say that. Let's re-examine this."

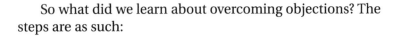
So what did we learn about overcoming objections? The steps are as such:

1. **Pause.**

2. **Relax.**

3. **Empathize.**

4. **Probe.**

5. **Playback.**

6. **Avoid self-imposed objections.**

7. **Solve.**

People buy on emotion. If emotions are not expressed, objections do not exist. If objections do not exist and a person does not buy at that moment, the sale will never be made.

CHAPTER 9

Network

Networking: The developing of long-term relationships
based on a mutual exchange of information to help
skyrocket incomes for at least two individuals

*Giving and receiving ideas to help improve one's own
business, giving and receiving support to help improve
one's attitude, and giving and receiving contacts to
further position oneself as a "sustaining resource" are all
networking.*

Why are the best salespeople always the best networkers? It's because networking is more than swapping leads and closing deals, as is selling. Networking is building relationships based on mutual trust. It's two individuals helping one another to ultimately make more money through the exchange of information.

Networking does not involve companies. It involves individuals. When you network properly, both parties agree to dedicate themselves to helping one another regardless of their companies. More importantly, networking involves helping others first, then seeking help for yourself.

In this chapter, we will present the playbook for how to network:

1. Understand what it takes to network.

2. Decide with whom to network.

3. Introduce.

4. Probe.

5. State Initial Benefit.

6. Commit to "coffee."

7. Send thank you via e-mail.

8. Call to schedule appointment.

9. Send PAL.

10. Conduct appointment.

11. Give lead via e-mail.

12. Correspond monthly.

Understand what it takes to network

Everybody claims to network. But to network effectively, you must have a certain mindset – a mindset that translates into executable behavior.

While your goal in reading this book is to make money for you and your company, the information you gain is yours. It will last you the rest of your life. The same can be said for networking. When you leave your company, you will take your ideas, contacts and networking relationships with you. It would be great to think you will stay at your company for the next 10 years, but the cold hard truth is that sales is a volatile industry. You are making an investment in reading this book – even if your company footed the bill. Networking is just as personal.

What does it take to network?

Be organized

From here on, treat every person you encounter like a prospect. Give them the same respect, courtesy and attention you would give those who may buy your services. Follow-up with them regularly.

Next, incorporate networking directly into your weekly schedule, as discussed earlier. Know which days you will network and what events you will attend. Sends PALs as you would to prospects.

Lead, persist and be patient

Be the one to take the first step. Introduce yourself first, offer to grab a "cup of coffee" first and volunteer leads first. As you would with a prospect, share your "ideal client" criteria and ask new networking friends the ideal criteria for their clients. But be patient. Results take time. The more you give, the more you receive.

Persistence, perseverance and patience will equal payoff.

Be selfish

The word "selfish" is one of the most misunderstood words in the English language. By definition, it means "taking care of the self." Despite its popular negative connotation, most of us agree that taking care of ourselves is very important. Only when we take care of ourselves first are we able to truly take care of others.

When people give to charity, we praise their generosity. "Isn't that great?" we say. "They aren't selfish." But the real reason people give is to receive. What they receive is that special glow caused by the satisfaction of giving.

The most selfish people in the world are the ones who donate millions to charity anonymously. They donate because they want to be rewarded with that wonderful feeling of having helped. They don't want to share that feeling.

Networking is the same way. When you are selfish, you will give and give and give because you understand it will help you. You will get more leads. You will get more clients. You will make more money.

"It is one of the most beautiful compensations of life that no man can sincerely try to help another without helping himself."

Ralph Waldo Emerson

Decide with whom to network

Earlier we discussed the importance of identifying your ideal client. In networking your concerns are the same. To make the most of networking, identify those who can help you the most – and those who you can help most. Usually, they are the same people. Don't get caught up in the Chamber of Commerce or leads groups unless those people target the same accounts you target or represent the types of accounts you want as customers. Networking is dangerous because, if you aren't careful, you can get involved in making a lot of friends without generating a lot of business.

It's not necessary to grab a cup of coffee with everyone. If you are in doubt as to whether you and your new friend can help one another, it's worth erring on the side of meeting.

When in doubt, meet out.

Be selective. Even though everyone should be entered in your database, some people can help you more than others, just as there are people you can help more than others.

How do you decide who is the person who can best help you? What you have in common in your businesses is the best measurement.

Here are some good questions to consider.

What type of person is an ideal networker for you?

- Do they want to network with you?
- Do they target the same accounts as you?
- Do they have the same sales territory?
- Does their product complement yours (i.e., phone equipment and phone service)?
- Do you feel comfortable referring business to them? (Their actions are a direct reflection – positive or negative – on you. If you are concerned they will not follow up promptly, don't refer them business. Since you are a professional, it will be a poor reflection on you if you refer an amateur.)
- Do they feel comfortable referring you?
- Do they sell the same way as you? (Are they passive and calm? Or are they aggressive and persistent?)
- Do you have similar personality traits?
- Are you similar in age? (Sometimes, this is good. Sometimes, it's not. Think about it.)
- Are your companies similar in size?
- Do you sell the same product but with different targets? (Competitors can be great sources as long as you target different size accounts)
- Can you learn from them? Will they make you a better salesperson?

Once you know the kinds of people with whom you want to network, determine where to find them. There are two types of networking:

- Formal
- Informal

Formal networking

Formal networking occurs at "official" functions. These include association meetings, Chamber of Commerce luncheons, After Hours and industry events. Everyone attends these events to make contacts. They can garner results, but they can be challenging. In essence, they are one big sales pitch. Everyone is selling everyone. The winner is usually the person who gives the most leads and asks the most questions.

Informal networking

Informal networking includes networking with friends, family, other health club members, etc. It is often frightening because you must be proactive in initiating contacts. You also must overcome the fear you are intruding or stepping on people's toes. But you may get your best clients going this route.

The following page suggests people with whom you might want to network. (Notice that it is almost the same list as those people with whom you would seek referrals.)

Who should you network with?

- Customers
- Prospects
- Friends/Relatives
- Internal employees
- Vendors
- Office equipment vendor
- Office supplies vendor
- Your accountant
- Your attorney
- Your insurance agent
- Your local, long distance, cellular phone, web hosting, internet provider
- Your health club
- Your landlord/condo association
- Your barber
- Your grocery store manager
- Your dry cleaner
- Members of Associations in which you or company have memberships
- Members of Chambers of Commerce in which you or company have memberships
- Members of Chambers of Commerce in area in which you live (even without membership)
- Leads groups (where weekly meetings are held and lead exchange is required)
- High School and College Alumni organizations
- Previous employers
- Past internal employees from previous employers
- Previous prospective employers
- Competitors (You all have your own unique niche)
- Salespeople who sell to the same clients in the same territory, but with a different product
- Salespeople who sell a complementary product in the same industry (for example, phone equipment vendors refer phone service providers)

Introduce

How you introduce yourself will often determine if a networking opportunity will be created. Whether in an informal or formal networking situation, get in the habit of introducing yourself in the following way:

- Firm handshake

- Smile

- Ask them their name

- Repeat their name, say your name

Probe

One of the biggest differences between networking and prospecting is that when you network, you do not say what you do until other people ask. First, find out what they do. Ask questions. Like on sales calls, you will automatically endear yourself. In addition, the more you probe, the guiltier other people feel about not knowing what you do. You are so busy being concerned about how you can help them that your own needs have become secondary. They see this. It will reach a point where they will say, "I'm sorry. We've been so busy talking about me. What do you do?" Here are suggested questions to ask before you even say what your job is:

- "What do you do?"

- "How long have you been doing it and how'd you get involved?"

- "What do you think has been the biggest key to your success?"

- "What's your biggest challenge?"

- "Who is the best client for you?"

State Initial Benefit

You've asked so many good questions that, at long last, the person with whom you are speaking can't wait to hear what you do. When that person asks, it's show time! You have this person's undivided attention. Now it's time for that amazing "initial benefit statement." Never say, "I sell phone service." Give them your best initial benefit statement as you did back in the Prospecting chapter. Then pause. Wait for a reaction.

Ideally, this person will ask more questions. Be careful. This is your time to sell yourself. The best way to sell yourself is by making the conversation about them, not you. Answer all their questions, but relate them back to what they said when they shared information about their business. Like we discussed earlier, build alliances to tie them back later.

Commit to "coffee"

Effective networking is not completed in a two-minute conversation. It requires an extensive in-person discussion to learn more about one another and how you can help one another. When you think you have enough information about this individual and that you are in a position to mutually benefit, cease the conversation by politely saying you would like to talk more at another time. If you don't think a future meeting would help further either of your businesses, politely excuse yourself. If it's a formal event, ask where the bathroom is, say that you'd like some food or simply indicate you'd like to "walk around."

But if you would like to get to know this person better, try to commit to a date and time right then and there. Pull out your datebook and schedule an appointment on the spot. Don't be too aggressive, but let them know you mean business. If you have the opportunity to avoid a possible game of phone tag, do so.

Send thank you via e-mail

Don't phone immediately. Even in informal networking situations, you are not the only person on the other person's mind. You may think you just had an amazing impact on this person, but the feeling may not be reciprocated. By tomorrow this person may not even remember what you discussed.

Remind them via e-mail including attachments with your basic company information (such as "What [Your Company] Can Do For You," "References," "Client List" and "Your Profile") as outlined earlier. Then say you will call on a certain day. If the synergy was not sufficient to make you want to schedule another meeting with this person, send an e-mail that concludes with "I look forward to speaking with you in the near future." Include your business information.

The following pages include templates for various kinds of letters.

Networking/Potential Business Thank You Letter

Subject: Skyrocketing sales for XXX – Basketball friend/TBN Sales Solutions President Todd Natenberg says great meeting you

So-and-So,

It was great meeting you recently at the ZZZ. Now, I've seen everything: earning potential business in the locker room with a terrific basketball player who at one time wanted to kick my butt because he "called" for the basketball? How funny is that? Ah, the power of networking.

Per our discussion, I have enclosed some basic information on my company, TBN Sales Solutions.

After you have had a chance to review the materials, I welcome the opportunity to sit down with you in person to discuss how TBN Sales Solutions will skyrocket sales for you and your reps at XXX. If nothing else, I'd welcome a networking discussion.

I will call you on Monday to schedule a mutually convenient date and time.

In the interim, I also encourage you to visit my website at www.toddnatenberg.com.

To reiterate, TBN Sales Solutions increases commissions for salespeople and profits for businesses through customized training, coaching and consulting. We establish structures and procedures in all facets of the sales process, through classroom workshops and individual sales coaching, to teach reps to control their own destinies, to impact the bottom line.

Please call (773) 755-1306 with questions or drop me an e-mail at todd@toddnatenberg.com. Otherwise, I look forward to speaking with you on Monday.

Sincerely,
Todd Natenberg
President

TBN Sales Solutions
711 W. Gordon Terrace, Ste. 106
Chicago, IL 60613
Phone: 773-755-1306, Fax: 773-442-0840, Outside Chicago: 866-464-0339
e-mail: todd@toddnatenberg.com
http://www.toddnatenberg.com

TBN Sales Solutions increases commissions for salespeople and profits for businesses through customized training, coaching and consulting. We establish structures and procedures in all facets of the sales process, through classroom workshops and individual sales coaching, to teach reps to control their own destinies, to impact the bottom line.

Networking/No Interest Thank You Letter

Subject: Skyrocketing sales for XXX, Chamber of Commerce Friend/TBN Sales Solutions President Todd Natenberg says great meeting you

So-and-So,

It was great meeting you recently at the Chamber of Commerce event. I enjoyed our discussion very much. I hope you received as much out of the event as I did.

Per our conversation, I have enclosed some additional materials further detailing my company, TBN Sales Solutions. I also encourage you to visit my website at www.toddnatenberg.com for the latest and greatest on our programs.

While I know we are in different worlds, should you hear of any companies or organizations looking for top-notch sales trainers, please keep me in mind. I'd greatly appreciate the support. Feel free to contact me at (773) 755-1306 or drop me an e-mail at todd@toddnatenberg.com. Likewise, I will do the same if I come across anyone who might want your services.

Just to reiterate, TBN Sales Solutions increases commissions for salespeople and profits for businesses through customized training, coaching and consulting. We establish structures and procedures in all facets of the sales process, through classroom workshops and individual sales coaching, to teach reps to control their own destinies.

Thanks again for the help. It was great meeting you.

I look forward to speaking with you in the near future.

Sincerely,
Todd Natenberg
President

TBN Sales Solutions
711 W. Gordon Terrace, Ste. 106
Chicago, IL 60613
Phone: 773-755-1306, Fax: 773-442-0840, Outside Chicago: 866-464-0339
e-mail: todd@toddnatenberg.com
http://www.toddnatenberg.com

TBN Sales Solutions increases commissions for salespeople and profits for businesses through customized training, coaching and consulting. We establish structures and procedures in all facets of the sales process, through classroom workshops and individual sales coaching, to teach reps to control their own destinies, to impact the bottom line.

Schedule appointment

Like prospecting, call on the day you promised to schedule a meeting. Pick a place that is out of the office for both of you. Offices can cause tension because expectations sometimes differ. Are you trying to help one another or are you selling one another? Coffee shops and bookstores are neutral places to meet.

Contrary to conventional practices, lunch is not recommended. When you meet over lunch, both parties focus on eating. Neither can fully pay attention to the subjects at hand. Taking notes and utilizing visuals is cumbersome.

When you eat lunch during a meeting, you fill your stomach, not your pocketbook.

Another reason you want to schedule the appointment, rather than having someone call you, is that now you can pick the location as well as the time. Fit the appointment into one of the time slots that has been allocated for networking based on the schedule you created in the Schedule chapter.

Send PAL

When was the last time someone received an agenda for a networking meeting? By sending the PAL, you set yourself above the rest. You take networking just as seriously as you take a true sales call. Who wouldn't want to network with you?

As indicated earlier, the agenda is different in a networking meeting, but the other items remain the same: confirmation, location, time limit, etc.

Conducting the appointment

Running a networking meeting is identical to running a sales call. The only difference is that you talk in terms of your fellow networker's "associates" or "clients." You are not trying to close the person in front of you. But you are trying to get the wheels rolling in terms of how that person can refer you.

One of the biggest mistakes people make on a networking call is forgetting that they are there to conduct business. Networking is just a different kind of business. Although probing is very similar to an ordinary sales call, two great questions to ask that may not come up on a normal sales call are:

- "Who is the ideal client for you? This way I know how I can refer you business."

- "How can I help you?"

We discussed defining the ideal client earlier in the chapter. It's good to ask it again on the coffee visit even though you asked it when you first met. It's still effective because it emphasizes your interest in networking.

Asking how you can help the person is done for a different reason. Often, while on a networking call, the person sitting across from you could be a prospect. But you don't want to try to "close" that person. This question measures whether that person is interested in your services without asking outright. For instance, the answer to "how can I help you?" could be one of two: 1)"If you come across clients looking for ..." or 2) "I'm not really sure, but I do think my company may need your services ..."

TBN Sales Solutions has earned more than one client that way.

Give leads via e-mail

Like in a prospect meeting, your goal in a networking
meeting is to advance the sales process. But the rules of
engagement differ. Typically, you will not schedule another firm
date and firm time. There may be no reason. But to keep the
process moving, one of you must take the next step. Be the first
to take it. The best way is by giving leads.

Networking leads do not have to only be for clearly defined
clients. Leads for information – or leads for other people to
network with – all count as leads, too. To make a lead most
effective, don't just tell your friend to call somebody. Think big!
Let everyone involved know what you are doing. Have a three-
way conversation via e-mail. Everyone will appreciate it: your
client, the referrer and the person with whom you are
networking. The following pages include templates for
networking leads.

Giving Networking Referral Letter

Subject: Skyrocketing sales for So-and-So and Company XXX, Chamber of Commerce Friend/TBN Sales Solutions President Todd Natenberg says thanks for meeting with me. REFERRAL to AAA, BBB, CCC
CC: ZZZ

So-and-So,

It was great speaking with you recently about TBN Sales Solutions and your own potential entry into the sales training industry. I appreciate you reaching out to me. I know we will speak more tomorrow, but in the interim, I wanted to offer you some suggestions and contacts to get you going.

Per our conversation, I credit much of my success to several terrific people I have corresponded with over the past couple of years who belong to an organization called the National Speakers Association. I've enclosed contact information for the executive director, AAA. I also included the names of a few members, including BBB and CCC. These people are committed to the training/speaking profession. They are great resources and offer wonderful advice and guidance. Likewise, they know better than anybody the power of networking.

AAA and BBB are pretty accessible. CCC is sometimes hard to reach, but I included his information because he is one of the best one-man operations for sales training. He's tops on the scale by which we measure ourselves. He's where we all want to be, having done this for quite some time and growing his business each year despite the bad economy.

All have hearts of gold!

(AAA, BB, and CCC, So-and-So is a friend of mine from my sales days at AT&T. He wants to get into sales training. He's charismatic, enthusiastic and has a natural curiosity. He'd be a great addition to the speaking profession.)

Giving Networking Referral Letter (cont.)

Here's everyone's contact information:

AAA	BBB
Company Name	Company Name
Phone #	Phone #
E-mail	E-mail
Website	Website
CCC	So-and-So
Company Name	Company XXX
Phone #	Phone #
E-mail	E-mail
Website	Website

Good luck to all! Keep me posted.

Please call (773) 755-1306 or e-mail todd@toddnatenberg.com with questions.

Sincerely,
Todd Natenberg
President

TBN Sales Solutions
711 W. Gordon Terrace, Ste. 106
Chicago, IL 60613
Phone: 773-755-1306, Fax: 773-442-0840, Outside Chicago: 866-464-0339
e-mail: todd@toddnatenberg.com
http://www.toddnatenberg.com

TBN Sales Solutions increases commissions for salespeople and profits for businesses through customized training, coaching and consulting. We establish structures and procedures in all facets of the sales process, through classroom workshops and individual sales coaching, to teach reps to control their own destinies, to impact the bottom line.

Potential Client Referral Letter

Subject: Impacting the bottom line for XXX – Todd Natenberg, TBN Sales Solutions, refers BBB, Company CCC, to help

So-and-So,

Hope all's well.

I know we needed to take a pass on TBN Sales Solutions as a training resource – for the moment – but I may be able to help you in another way. You know I always pride myself on being a sustaining resource to XXX – whether by offering phone service, sales training, etc.

With your permission, I am passing along your contact information to a business associate of mine – BBB of Company CCC. I recall a while back you had indicated you were not entirely pleased with your current vendor in this area. BBB is sharp as a tack and may be in a position to help you with financial business services. I don't know exactly where you are in terms of your bank relationships, but it's definitely worth a conversation. BBB targets companies of your size. Expect his call in the next week.

(BBB, likewise, So-and-So is one of the oldest and best clients of TBN Sales Solutions. We go way back. He is as loyal as they come – if you can provide what you promise. I know you can. Otherwise, I would not be recommending you).

For all involved, here's everyone's contact information:

Good luck to all! Keep me posted. Happy selling!

BBB	So-and-So
Company CCC	Company XXX
Phone #	Phone #
E-mail	E-mail
Website	Website

Sincerely,
Todd Natenberg
President

TBN Sales Solutions
711 W. Gordon Terrace, Ste. 106 Chicago, IL 60613
Phone: 773-755-1306, Fax: 773-442-0840, Outside Chicago: 866-464-0339
e-mail: todd@toddnatenberg.com http://www.toddnatenberg.com

TBN Sales Solutions increases commissions for salespeople and profits for businesses through customized training, coaching and consulting. We establish structures and procedures in all facets of the sales process, through classroom workshops and individual sales coaching, to teach reps to control their own destinies, to impact the bottom line.

Correspond monthly

If you don't keep in touch with people you are networking with, there is no point in networking. E-mail is once again the route to go. Add your new networking contacts to your newsletter list. At the minimum, there must be some touch once a month. A voice mail is good every two months.

Do's and don'ts of networking

- Always have business cards with you

No excuses. Keep business cards in your briefcase, all athletic bags, your wallet, your car and in your desk at work. Always have at least 10. Have minimum of 30 when attending a formal networking event. You never know when or where opportunities will surface. Napkins with e-mails and phone numbers get lost easily.

- Have e-mail on your business card

This may sound trite, but there are still people without e-mail addresses listed on their business cards. In this day and age, there is no excuse for not having an e-mail address on your card. E-mail is an integral tool if you are in sales. How can you network with someone who does not know how to reach you?

- Give a card/get a card

Some people say handing out two cards is ideal, because the recipient will keep one and give one to a prospect for you. The idea is solid, but the practice creates clutter. Also, assuming someone wants to refer you business without knowing much about you or what you can do can be a big turnoff. Once you conduct the initial appointment on neutral turf, hand out a stack of cards to your new ally.

- Always have pen and paper

You'd be amazed how many people don't have something to write with. Ideally, you'll take notes on the business card you just received. If you need more space, have paper handy. No one expects you to remember everything, but the more information you can reference, the stronger your position.

- Always have your date book

If you can avoid phone tag and e-mail tag, do. Always be prepared to schedule an appointment. Let the other person look unprofessional.

- Don't interrupt – even if you want to leave

Graciously wait for a pause to exit the conversation if you think it's not worth continuing.

If you're attending a formal event, the following also apply:

- Introduce yourself to the host of the event.

- Introduce yourself to the speaker of the event, if time permits.

- If you're attending a meal, don't worry about eating. You're there to network. Eat beforehand.

What did we learn about networking? The steps in networking are these:

1. Understand what it takes to network.

2. Decide with whom to network.

3. Introduce.

4. Probe.

5. State Initial Benefit.

6. Commit to "coffee."

7. Send thank you via e-mail.

8. Call to schedule appointment.

9. Send PAL.

10. Conduct appointment.

11. Give lead via e-mail.

12. Correspond monthly.

Networking is about finding opportunities and having opportunities found for you. It's about developing long-standing relationships that mutually benefit you – and those around you. Help others and you will be helped.

CHAPTER 10

Professional Development

Professional Development: The continuous exploration
of new ideas to implement in daily sales

*When we stop growing, we stop dreaming. When we stop
dreaming, we stop living life to the fullest.*

Why is it that the most successful people in the world always credit their success to others? Great presidents have great advisers, great athletes have great coaches, and great business people have great mentors. Do you notice a pattern?

To truly be successful, ongoing improvement is a must. It's no surprise that often salespeople's biggest slumps come after their biggest successes. They think they know it all, rest on their laurels and forget to constantly improve. Don't stop learning.

In 1998, *Time Magazine* wrote a cover story about how Tiger Woods reinvented his swing shortly after winning the Masters tournament. He worked on his swing with his coach while he was ranked the top golfer in the world!

For the next year or so, you did not hear much about Tiger. He won his share of tournaments and was still ranked Number One. But the year after, Tiger's career reached unimaginable heights. He won what is now known as the Tiger Slam, four major golf tournaments held consecutively over a one-year period.

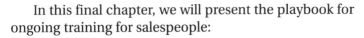
In this final chapter, we will present the playbook for ongoing training for salespeople:

1. Improve your own buying habits.

2. Watch other selling habits.

3. Read.

4. Utilize classroom sales training.

5. Take risks.

Improve your own buying habits

Throughout this book, we have repeatedly emphasized "sell how you want to buy." If you are an impulsive buyer, you will be an impulsive seller. If you are a meticulous buyer, you may be a meticulous seller.

Impulsive sellers usually do not fear asking for the order. They have a sense of urgency which will transmit itself to the buyer.

Meticulous sellers, however, are often reluctant to ask for orders (or even to advance the sales process). They empathize that if they were the buyer, they probably would not buy the product on the first appointment. Meticulous sellers sometimes delay the sales process unnecessarily.

Often they tell their managers, "I can't be pushy like that. I can't do that to the customer." They wouldn't be "doing" anything – they'd be earning a client. However, they may not view it that way.

While styles vary, to succeed in sales certain personality traits must be stressed, including persistence, confidence and perseverance. Though the execution of the sale may vary, the required characteristics are the same for each transaction.

So the question is: How do we improve our buying habits – if we should at all?

Improvement begins with awareness. If you are a meticulous buyer, it doesn't mean you have to suddenly start buying impulsively. It just means you must recognize this as a limitation in your selling habits. One of the best ways to recognize this is to pay closer attention when you purchase items. Notice what you like about the salesperson when you buy. Notice the result of your own practices. Why do you buy? What do you buy? You'll be amazed at the similarities between selling clothes in a store and selling a $10,000 product. To illustrate this point, let's conduct an exercise involving negotiating at a retail store. The results will astound you.

BUYING HABITS EXERCISE

For this exercise to work, the following steps must be followed:

- Prepare

Be prepared to make a little scene. People may stare. You won't be rude or embarrassing, but you may draw attention. Expect it.

- Introduce yourself to a salesperson

Find a salesperson to help you. Ask the salesperson's name and, with a firm handshake, introduce yourself. State the person's name once again adding, "Nice to meet you, So-and-So. I was wondering if you could help me."

You probably are the first person in the last six months – or ever – to actually ask salespeople their names, let alone treat them with respect. They will be flattered more than you can ever imagine.

- Request the manager by asking for "help"

Don't waste your time talking to someone who can't reduce the price. This is the one time when you skip the gatekeeper. Retail salespeople often are guaranteed to say "no" because they can't say "yes."

Retail salespeople usually have no vested interest in whether you purchase the item. Their hourly wage is unaffected by your purchase. But someone in that store does care. With the salesperson's help, you need to get to that person. As you've already been respectful, this shouldn't be an issue. But you do have to stand firm. Here's how it works:

You:	"So-and-so. I'd like to speak to the manager please. I have a question about this item."
Salesperson:	"What is it? Perhaps I can answer it."
You:	"No, I appreciate that, but I'd like to speak to the manager. Thanks for your *help*."

• Introduce yourself to manager/Ask for help

The manager is expecting an angry customer, because why else would someone ask for the manager? Your salesperson may have explained you are not a lunatic (you were very courteous to the salesperson) but still, managers are usually called to address problems. Watch the manager's surprise when you are calm, pleasant and actually compliment the salesperson who helped you.

You:	"Are you the manager?"
Manager:	"Yes."
You:	"What's your name? My name's Todd. *(shake hands.)* It's nice to meet you, So-and-So. I was speaking with salesperson So-and-So, who was very helpful. But I had a question for you. I was wondering if you could *help* me, too."
Manager:	"Well, that depends. What can I do for you?"

You now have the manager's undivided attention. The manager might suspect you will ask him to reduce the price, but you have approached it professionally and politely. Also, you may be the first one to ever have done it this way. At this point the manager is wishing more buyers would act like you.

What have you done thus far? You have actually not asked for a thing, but you have complimented the employee, the manager and the store overall.

- Probe

Now you need to create a reason why the manager should lower the price. But don't ask for a price reduction outright. Leave it open a little to speculation. The speculation will arise from your questions. Your argument may not be strong, but do make an argument. Some examples include:

> "Does this ever go on sale? Oh, it does? Since I'm here now, is there any chance you could help me? I don't want to be watching the ads for the next few months. I'd really appreciate the *help*."

> "It's more than I wanted to spend. I shop here all the time. Can you *help* me?"

> "I've seen it for less elsewhere. It's really the one I want. I shop here all the time. Can you *help* me?"

Notice the "Can you help me?" comment. You haven't actually asked for a price reduction, although you've implied it. If the manager seems confused about what you're asking, continue, saying, "Can you help me out on the price?"

At this point, one of a few things will happen:

- "The price is what it is. Sorry about that," the manager says.

- Or … success!

But assuming neither of these reactions occur, there is a third and more common reaction – silence. If this is the response, say nothing. The manager is now thinking about your request. If you interrupt, you are dead in the water.

- Challenge

If you don't succeed, don't be confrontational. Challenge the manager's answers, but only to a degree. If you get the discount, it won't be because of your argument. It will be because the manager likes you based on the other steps you took.

If you say you've seen it for less elsewhere, the manager might suggest that you bring in the ad so the store can honor the competition's price. Don't let it get to that point. You will lose all credibility. Here's a recommendation:

> "I appreciate that, So-and-So, but I admit I
> don't have the ad. I don't even know if it was
> the same item or when it was on sale. It was
> similar. That's all I know. Can you *help* me
> out?"

- Thank the manager

If you succeed in getting the discount, whatever the discount is, take it. You are miles ahead of everyone else. Be happy. If you don't succeed, that's still okay. Thank the manager anyway. Proceed to the register, assuming you meant to buy the item in the first place. Your goal was not really to save money, although that's a nice benefit when this works! You were really practicing being the buyer.

The other reason to thank the manager no matter what the outcome is that you have not yet walked out the door. You never know what might happen by the time you get to the register.

Not only have I been successful with this exercise more than 50% of the time, but there have been some occasions when the manager followed me to the payment counter and then gave me a discount. The manager was so shocked by my sincerity, he couldn't resist helping me – after I already agreed to buy the item at full price!

- Additional thank you upon exit

Even if you do not get a discount, find the manager and salesperson and thank them. You will feel better. So will they.

Watch other selling habits

The next time you purchase items, observe the sellers. Ask yourself questions. What do you like about them? What don't you like? Do you like if they talk fast? Do you like if they talk slow? Why do salespeople never ask your name? How does it make you feel when they do? When they ask if they can "help" you, how does that sound?

Recently I was at a restaurant when the cashier said, "Can I help the next guest?" We know the power of the word "help." How did "guest" make me feel? Pretty good, I must admit.

Here's another example. Rob is my realtor and has become a close personal friend. I was one of Rob's first sales when he sold me my condominium. Two months after moving in, he asked me for a letter of recommendation. "I have a favor to ask of you. I need your help," he said. I wrote the letter on the spot.

The following page suggests people in occupations you know. Think about them in terms of their selling skills. What do you like about them … and what don't you like about them? What characteristics can you isolate that influence how you feel about them? What characteristics do they have that relate to their selling skills?

Who can serve as a model to learn good – and bad – selling skills?

Accountants	Lawyers
Athletes in interviews	Maintenance workers
Bus drivers	Movie actors
CEO of your company	Police officer
Customer service representatives	Politicians
Disc jockeys	Priests/Rabbis/Minister
Doctor	Professional athletes
Dry cleaner	Restaurant manager
Family	Restaurant server
Fireman	Sales director
Friends	Sales manager
Fundraising telemarketers	Salespeople at other companies
Grocery clerk	Salespeople at your company
Guests on talk shows	School teachers
Hair Stylists	School principals
Help desk	Social worker
Journalists	Talk show hosts
Judges	Taxi driver
Landlord	Television actors/actresses

Read

Those who read are those who lead.

Someone once said that a book is a combination of a writer's persona and expertise, wrapped into a portable package you can carry with you. You can access that author whenever you want just by opening the book. Television may be entertaining and informative, but don't neglect books, newspapers, newsletters and periodicals. Commit to being a lifelong learner. Read at least one book every two months. Pick whatever titles interest you, but include some business books in your selection.

Read your local city newspaper, business magazines and selling magazines. Pick those that are most interesting for you. For the sake of time, here's a shortcut I recommend when reading newspapers or magazine. Read first:

- The headlines

- The table of contents

- The front page and the back page

There also are some terrific free publications on the internet. Virtually all newspapers enable you to receive free headlines on a daily basis. Wherever you live, subscribe via e-mail to your local newspaper. Investigate E-zines. Pick and choose the ones you find most appropriate. You can't beat the price and the ease. Take advantage of your computer.

Classroom sales training

While often the best training comes in the field, don't discount the value of the classroom. Strategic theory is very useful. Theory enables you to bounce ideas off colleagues, experts and others you respect. Isn't that why you are reading this book? The type of sales training you select is up to you. But be sure you actively train at least one day a month. Keep your skills fresh in a group environment. If your manager won't pay for training, pay for it yourself. It's worth it in the long run. One full day a month, at least, is recommended.

Take risks

By nature, salespeople must take risks. Any time you cold call a prospect, any time you ask for an order, any time you pick up the phone, you are risking someone refusing you. The fact is 99% of salespeople's job involves others refusing your ideas. But notice the words. It's not rejection. It's not failure. It's a refusal of your ideas – actually your services.

Encompass your selling philosophy in your everyday life. Take risks. Try new things. Make a pact with yourself, here and now, that once a month you will try something new. You pick the specific activity, but let it be something that before you read this book, you wouldn't try.

Life's lessons come from daily events. But our greatest lessons come from things that we do not experience every day.

Let's recap our guide to professional development.

1. **Improve your own buying habits.**

2. **Watch other selling habits.**

3. **Read.**

4. **Utilize classroom sales training.**

5. **Take risks.**

When we stop getting better, we cease being good.

Conclusion

When we first began this journey, I promised that you would receive at least 10 concrete strategies and selling tools you could implement into your job tomorrow. Did you?

In summary, the 10 Step Selling Process is:

1. **Set Goals**

2. **Schedule**

3. **State Initial Benefit**

4. **Prospect**

5. **Obtain Referrals**

6. **Build the Business Case**

7. **Follow-up**

8. **Overcome Objections**

9. **Network**

10. **Professional Development**

Congratulations! You are now among the elite: The Salesperson. You are the best of the best. When you achieve in sales, you achieve in all aspects of your life. Sales is a direct reflection of the world in which we live.

Life is filled with ups and down. The key is to cherish those peaks and survive those valleys. Selling is no different.

But we must never forget what it takes for us to succeed. When we recognize our formula for success, it's critical we repeat and repeat again. It's a never ending circle, one in which we love and will continue to love. It is through our process, our playbook, our grand plan that when executed enables us to achieve all we want, all we desire, and all we deserve.

Just ask journalist John where he is today and where he would be, had he not decided to enter the sales profession. Did John make the right decision?

I think I can answer that one for him: All I need to do is look in the mirror to know the answer: Yes!

Welcome to sales!

Index

Want TBN Sales Solutions Live?

Todd Natenberg
President

TBN Sales Solutions increases commissions for salespeople and profits for businesses through customized training, coaching and consulting. We establish structures and procedures in all facets of the sales process, through classroom workshops and individual sales coaching, to teach reps to control their own destinies, to impact the bottom line.

TBN programs range from 5-days to 1/2 day and include the following topics:

- *Goal Setting and Time Management*
- *Prospecting*
- *Running a Sales Call*
- *Objection Handling*
- *Networking*
- *Team Building*
- *Leadership*
- *Maintenance*

In addition, TBN develops customized sales tools and provides consultative services in the following areas:

- Written Assessments/Recommendations
- Ride Alongs
- Individual Sales Coaching

All TBN Services include:

- *FREE* monthly subscription to *Skyrocketing Sales Solutions!* (TBN Sales Solution's newsletter)

- *FREE* advertisement on www.toddnatenberg.com

- *FREE* access to Todd's network (with more than 10,000 contacts)

Company packages and follow-up visits also are available.

TBN brings a unique approach to the sales training process. Combining humor with personal and professional success stories, President Todd Natenberg pulls from all facets of life to teach the art of selling. A self-described "facilitator," his programs are extremely interactive and entertaining. From Hollywood movies to newspaper articles to traditional role plays, nothing is out of bounds for Todd. Past students describe him as "charismatic, energetic and a true professional."

For more information on TBN Sales Solutions, please call (773) 755-1306 or e-mail todd@toddnatenberg.com. Also please visit us on the web at www.toddnatenberg.com.

Praise for TBN Sales Solutions ...

"I always thought of myself as a good salesperson, but I wanted to become a great salesperson. I use a lot of the skills you showed me as second nature. The same skills have also helped me in my personal life, which is an added bonus. I truly believe in your training course and encourage all my loan officers to attend. Thanks for all your great help and effort."

Chuck Sowers, President, American Mortgage Werks, Inc.

"I've signed new consulting contracts and brought on new clients using techniques and ideas that you have taught. My overall approach to sales is much more structured and effective after having your sales coaching. I'll be honest. Initially, I was skeptical, but I can say now it well worth the time and money.

"I would highly recommend you to anyone wishing to get a better grasp of the sales process or to refine their marketing and sales strategy. "

Nathan Laurell, Partner, Technacity, LLC

"Your seminar was great. I was able to articulate my business message in a clear and concise manner for the first time. I learned new techniques. It also was a great review. Being a former sales manager, I know the importance of all three. Your seminar has enabled me to speed up the development of my new business. You are a tremendous facilitator and I would recommend you to anyone."

Paul Baraz, Director of Fun and Games, Actualization Enterprises, Strategic Organizational Interventions

"Since your first visit we have noticed heightened awareness of personal and professional goals, more employee conversation about teamwork, and more interaction between employees and management.

"Thanks again for the insight and inspiration which your leadership and team building training has provided our company. It has become a valuable asset to the way we do business at Wadsworth Pumps."

James Wadsworth, Director of Operations, Wadsworth Pumps, W.J. Wadsworth and Associates, Inc.,

(continued on next page)

"I would like to extend my heartfelt thanks for the outstanding presentation you presented to our management staff members. I can't tell you how energized our people were as a result of your program. I look forward to working with you in the future. Your passion, energy and commitment to helping people grow is inspiring."

Leslie Smigel, Property Manager, Century Point Luxury Apartment Homes

"Since participating in your seminars less than a month ago, we have had a record month in sales. The simple but powerful tools we learned have helped us gain a new momentum and will give us the confidence to maintain it. Thank you for putting together a great seminar series."

Alex Puig, CEO, Allied Computer Training Center

"The feedback I have received from our staff after your Time Management seminar was very positive. I don't write recommendation letters unless I see tangible results from my staff at least one to two months after any presentation. However, I just had a staff meeting, and sure enough, a large percentage of the staff are still using the time management techniques you presented at our corporate off site. I appreciated your presentation techniques, and I know the majority of the staff found your presentations entertaining and informative."

Mark J. Cleaver, CEO, Technomic International

"Your training was extremely beneficial and we have seen immediate results. Our new salespeople are scheduling twice as much activity as the initial results from some of our other training classes. Much of this success is a direct result of your hands on approach. The feedback from our sales force was very positive. They thought that your program was very interactive, as well as entertaining."

Paul Rosen, Vice President of Sales and Marketing, E-Chx, Inc.

"I liked having the opportunity to gather together as a group and discuss different tactics and methods. I liked best the role playing and then having everyone's evaluations. You were good. You helped everyone get involved."

Stephanie Urbanski, Account Executive, CyberSearch Ltd.

ALSO BY TODD NATENBERG ...

The Journey Within:
Two Months on Kibbutz

In the summer of 2000, Todd B. Natenberg, a 30-year-old resident of Chicago, quit his job as a sales manager and sales trainer, started his own sales training company, sold his house and finalized a divorce. But before embarking on his new career and his new life, he took the adventure he had always wanted: volunteering on an Israeli kibbutz.

By venturing to the most contentious of places and submersing himself in one of the world's oldest and richest cultures – his heritage – Todd teaches us about how true fulfillment comes from our connection with others.

The Journey Within: Two Months on Kibbutz is for anyone who has questioned the meaning of life.

"A personal journal of an intrepid individual with a big heart and open mind who dove in head first to learn a lot about himself and others. The Journey Within: Two Months on Kibbutz *is not so much a story about Israel. It's about relationships with others and the impact they have on us."*

Aaron Cohen
Editor, JUF News

"Where is a heart to feel from one's heart? In The Journey Within, *Todd Natenberg fearlessly recounts a journey that few of us are willing to undertake. It's exhilarating to go along for the ride."*

John Kador, author of *Charles Schwab: How One Company Beat Wall Street and Reinvented the Brokerage Industry*

"Todd is someone who loves and enjoys people. His thoughts on the kibbutz are fascinating. His insights into all those he met are very revealing. It's amazing how those he met could trigger such depths of emotions. We should all learn Todd's lessons."

Michael Wynne
Past President of National Speakers Association-Illinois

"A terrific book. The Journey Within: Two Months on Kibbutz *is not only Todd's story and his search for answers. It's also a wonderful insight into life on a kibbutz and the diverse people who live and work on it."*

Rita Emmett
Author of *The Procrastinator's Handbook: Mastering the Art of Doing It Now*

"In his journey to a kibbutz and his journey since, Natenberg has discovered that nothing feeds the soul like a small world made larger."

Brad Herzog
Author of *States of Mind* and *Small World*

Copies of *The Journey Within: Two Months on Kibbutz* can be purchased online where all fine books are sold or call 877-823-9235.

SKYROCKET YOUR SALES!!!!

**Yes, I want to order another copy of
"I just got a job in Sales Now what?"** $19.95

Special pricing on multiple copies!
2 to 10 copies – 20% discount $15.95/book
11 to 30 copies – 25% discount 14.95/book
31 to 50 copies – 30% discount 13.95/book

Mail to: _____

Address: _____

City: _____

St: _____ Zip Code: _____

IL residents, add 8.75% sales tax _____

Shipping and handling _____
*($4 for the first book;
$2 for each additional book)*

Total _____

Bill my credit card #: ❏ MasterCard ❏ Visa ❏ American Express

Card #: _____

Expiration Date: _____ 3-digit security code _____
(on back of card)

Signature _____

❏ Sign me up for the TBNSS newsletter,
Skyrocketing Sales Solutions!
My e-mail address is _____

To order
Call: 773.755.1306   Fax: 773.442.0840
www.ijustgotajobinsales.com
or mail to:
TBN Sales Solutions
711 West Gordon Terrace, Suite 106
Chicago, IL 60613

Notes

Notes